"An Incorruptible Heart"
Copyright © 2011 David McCracken
All rights reserved
Published by David McCracken Ministries,
Narre Warren North, Victoria, Australia.
National Library of Australia Cataloguing-in-Publication entry:
McCracken, David
An Incorruptible Heart : Having influence without losing your
integrity / David McCracken; cartoons by Brett Cardwell.
2nd edition
Christian leadership
Spiritual direction
ISBN: 978-0-9871314-1-6(pbk.)
DDC: 253.5

DAVID McCRACKEN

An

INCORRUPTIBLE

HEART

Having Influence Without Losing Your Integrity

ENDORSEMENTS

David McCracken's book "An Incorruptible Heart" is a must for any library – especially ministers and those in areas of leadership. David has written a number of books, but "An Incorruptible Heart - Having influence without losing your integrity" would be David's 'masterpiece' of all his works. In this text, more than others, he writes like he speaks. May the Lord bless this book to the Body of Christ.

Kevin J. Conner
International Author and Theologian, Australia

David McCracken is an amazing apostolic prophet for the 21st century. In his book 'An Incorruptible Heart' David shows his brilliant insight into all aspects of the Kingdom. I know as you read this book you will be inspired to live a life that has an incorruptible heart. This is a must read!

Russell Evans
Senior Pastor, Planetshakers City Church, Australia

David McCracken's excellent book reminds us of the power of an incorruptible heart. I often say, "don't trust a leader who doesn't limp." Meaning... people who have gone through the fires of trials, pressures, crisis, pain, and disappointment, yet have decided to trust God and be people of integrity with a sweet spirit. Those who limp have been there and have come out better. I listen to these people and learn. David is one of those people. His book is full of transparency, vulnerability, and wisdom arising from the pressures of ministry and life. Throughout his writing he brings hope, inspiration, and faith to us who are looking for positive examples. He reminds us of the critical truth that we must protect our heart from bitterness, walk the road of integrity, and keep tender to the things of God and to the needs of people. All of us have seen leaders who have compromised and become hardened, and wounded. David's message is that we can do all things in Christ, and we can trust God in our precious gift of ministry for His Kingdom.

Dr Wayde Goodall
Author, President WorldWideFamily.org, Colorado Springs, USA

This book 'An Incorruptible Heart' is deeply challenging. It is written out of the depths of experiences of life, ministry and significant Biblical understanding. It's uncomfortable to have the mirror turned on you as it is read. However, one feels inward renewal as one surrenders to the truth. In a fast moving Christian sub-culture it is worth making a priority read.

Ian Green
Visionary Leader, Next Level International, England

In all the years I've known David, whenever he has shared in person and in print it has been an overflow of revelation given to him by God, flowing from a life of prayer. Enjoy the impartation!

Ps Danny Guglielmucci
Senior Minister of Edge Church International

With so much tragic failure in Christian ministries and leadership today, how must we face the new millennium? David McCracken has done us all a great service in analysing and compiling the great themes of faithful leadership; servant hearts, yielded expectations, accountability and intimacy with Christ; utterly necessary principles for us to honor the Lord in the great decade of harvest before us. My Dad (a champion cyclist) once said to me: "Son, it's not how you begin the race; it's how you finish that counts." David's book will help you cross that line a winner!

Winkie Pratney
International Speaker and Author, USA

Refreshingly biblical, timely and to point... David McCracken is an impact player whose heart truly beats after God. He has taken on the undeniably crucial questions about integrity of church leadership and the human heart, and provides answers that point heavenward. This is a book of clarity. It seems fitting that David McCracken would write such a book. And why not? He is one who lives the integrity that he graciously holds up to others. How refreshing biblical... a God–centered perspective, on life, personal responsibility and leadership. David rescues biblical leadership from the hype of contemporary change and returns it to the desires of God's heart. This is a book of clarity.

Gary Ezzo
Director, Growing Families International, USA

Jesus came to change us from the inside out. This kind of deep personal transformation only takes place through the work of the Holy Spirit and through our co-operation. In this book, David McCracken unpacks some of the important issues related to our inner world, so that we can have a heart that pleases God. I highly recommend it.

Mark Conner
Senior Minister, CityLife Church, Australia

As I write I am sitting in a pediatric ward with my infant daughter. She is attached to different equipment and has had a barrage of tests and we wait a prognosis of what is causing the infection in her tiny body. We are confident it is not serious but we want to know. It strikes me rather precisely that this is exactly what this book is all about. Testing, trying, diagnosing and preventing harmful infection in the servants of God and therefore in the larger body of Christ. Why do good men go astray? Why do some of the most gifted ministries "lose the plot"? In his disarmingly straightforward way David McCracken once again opens us up like a skilled surgeon to ask ourselves "how did we get here" and "how do I avoid making the same mistake ?". I find his approach in this book humbling and a super calibrating tool. He speaks with wisdom gained by (often painful) experience - which is priceless. I would recommend anyone thinking of going into ministry and seasoned ministers to read this book and allow the Master Physician to use David's text as a "preventative medicine" so we can keep our hearts in top condition so that we can serve wholeheartedly and bring glory to God. David, this book is as vital to the minister as a stethoscope to a physician.

Christie Buckingham
Senior Pastor, Bayside Church

I have known David McCracken for over 14 yrs and have witnessed his amazing devotion to the development of leaders. His insight into God's desire for His people motivates this passion for the pursuit of excellence. I trust this book will inspire and challenge you as it has me, to raise your own awareness for the need of genuine integrity, especially as we see the Day of our Lord fast approaching. May God bless you abundantly as you absorb the principles sealed within the words of this book.

Dan Daniels
CEO Daniels Corporation

I have known David McCracken, for 35 years, and during that time, have not had any need to question his Integrity!!! In the writing of this book "An Incorruptible Heart" I know that David's desire would be for the reader to be open to hearing his heart. I have journeyed with David through the years, and it is my pleasure to know this friend of mine, whose heart can be trusted at all times.

John Steele
New Life Churches, New Zealand

In his book 'An Incorruptible Heart' David McCracken deals with an extremely needed message within the Body of Christ. Leaders have great influence over people, and carry an amazing responsibility before God and before society, hence not only we need gifted and charismatic leaders, but also those with a good dose of godly character and motivation. Drawing upon his extensive leadership experience as well as his ministry to leaders in all walks of life, David McCracken offers a clear and insightful teaching, with a transparent heart, making himself very often vulnerable. David's love and passion to see Leaders with a pure heart and pure motives in a society consumed by lust for power, pleasure and possession, is refreshing and encouraging teaching. I highly endorse this book.

Elio Marrocco
General Superintendant Canadian Assemblies of God, Canada

As I read this most excellent book, 'An Incorruptible Heart', and having had the privilege of knowing David and Margaret McCracken for around 30 years, this is their lives. It is easy to see that this book has been forged from the decades of ministry experienced by David, starting where we all start: young, zealous and naive to developing into very senior mature leadership. David's heart, his life, his experience, his blood sweat and tears are spilled onto these pages. What a book for Senior Pastors to keep us on the "straight and narrow" in order to achieve what we all set out for. What a book for existing leadership to keep the hearts right and save the "body" from the heartaches of the past. What a book for emerging leadership to forewarn them of the pitfalls that can await them. What a book for the body of Christ at large to help the saints, both young and old, to grow into the full measure and stature of Christ. This will be in our bookshop and will be a great read for all the leadership team here at City Impact Church. Thank-you David, and I love not only the practical, easy to read way you have in writing about the deeper issues of ministry but I also have to say I love the cartoons. Well done.

Ps Peter Mortlock
Senior Pastor City Impact Churches, New Zealand

It's always a joy (and challenge) to hear David teach or to read one of his books which all display a man in love with God. Like his biblical namesake, he has consistently sought to shepherd God's people "according to the integrity of his heart, and guided them by the skilfulness of his hands" (Psalm 78:72). This book is powerful testimony of that, succinctly cutting through much hype and paraphernalia that surrounds leadership to reveal the simplicity and purity of devotion towards God and others that flows from a humble and truly selfless heart. Again, David's prophetic insights give the book an urgency and an edge that insists we listen and respond in these "perilous times" if we want to be part of Christ's great last days' church (a church which many believe will be significantly different to much of what has gone before). These, coupled with the reflective questions at the end of each chapter make "An Incorruptible Heart" an inspired choice for individuals, small groups and leaders to work their way through as a tool to search their own heart motivations and to walk more intimately with Christ. Of course, for the most part this also requires God-hungry, Christ-centred leaders enabling it to be in the first place. I pray those hearts and this book will find each other.

Alan Stephenson
Founder & Director, The Joshua Foundation, Tanzania

In a day of fast tracking prominence or at least a desire for it, David McCracken speaks to us in 'An Incorruptible Heart', skilfully reminding us of our duty to slow the pace of our lives and develop disciplines long forgotten. We read in 2 Chronicles 12:1 what I think is one of the most frightful verses in the Bible "Now it came to pass, when Rehoboam had established the kingdom and had strengthened himself, that he forsook the law of the LORD, and all Israel along with him." David shows how a leader can have growing influence and even renown. But unless they keep and guard their heart at the same time, the end result might be devastating not only for the leader, but those around them.

Glenn Barker
Senior Minister, Life Church, England

I love good authors when they have the ability to deliver a great message that get to my heart. But David McCracken is with 'An Incorruptible Heart' more than a great author. Besides his ability to get the message across he has carried this message through in his life. It is the shaping *and moulding of God in David's life that have resulted in these great truths. David continues to live the content of this book out in everyday life. Because of that, many people in The Netherlands have received the sound and life changing message David brings. 'An Incorruptible Heart' is an outstanding tool in David's ministry to see the church all over the world empowered to become like Jesus in character and authority.*

David Koerts
Senior Pastor, Living Waters, Delft, The Netherlands

In his inspiring book, 'An Incorruptible Heart', David McCracken skilfully lays a solid foundation addressing key issues to spiritual success such as....loyalty, faithfulness, respect and integrity in the midst of trials and pressure. All the while he places top priority on advancing the kingdom with moral purity and godliness in every area of our lives. Each chapter builds towards a rewarding crescendo teaching its readers how to maintain a solid foundation of servanthood guarded by Godly character. This is a road worth travelling – complete reliance on the Holy Spirit and His plan for our lives as we walk in honour and cleanness to get to our final destination.

Marcus D. Lamb
Founder – President, Daystar Television Network, USA

Awesome book. Enjoyable to read , thought provoking and deeply challenging. Immensely readable and thoroughly practical advice to all who want to please the Father. David imparts timeless lessons with fiery freshness and sounds vital warnings for every leader!

Jim Shaw
Senior Pastor, Manukau New Life, New Zealand

A picture paints a thousand words. This book describes and paints a picture of Godly ways that is needed for a leader to lead God's people in God's ways.

Dr Rajan Thiagarajah
Senior Pastor, Mighty Living Waters Life Fellowship, Australia

THANK YOU

This book and the glimpses of my journey contained in it would have been a complete impossibility without the indescribable loyalty, love and deep spiritual strength of my wife, Margaret. She is my best friend and my greatest inspiration. To say I love her more now than ever is the understatement of the century!

Mark Butler has been an enormous help in creative suggestions, additional thoughts and rearrangements of the book. He just kept goading me to make it better. Thank you for that Mark.

Dariel Forlong did excellent proofreading and gave editing suggestions for which we are extremely grateful.

Special thanks also to Brett Cardwell (Cardy Toons) who so skilfully recreated many of the old cartoons I've used over the years and has done a brilliant job.

My personal assistant, Michelle, my son and "Elisha", Steve, and our DMM staff have constantly inspired me and their love and support ensured that a "good idea" become reality. So many aspects of this project are due to such an awesome team. My "Dream Team".

Above all, My Heavenly Father, whose grace, long suffering, forgiveness, perseverance and inexhaustible love has allowed me to run this race with integrity. The warmth of His embrace and the affirmation of His smile are life itself to me and the writing of this book is to honour Him.

CONTENTS

Prelude   xix

Introduction   xxiii

Chapter One: Love or Lust   1

Chapter Two: The Judas Spirit   19

Chapter Three: Intimacy   37

Chapter Four: Influence with Grace   53

Chapter Five: Servanthood   65

Chapter Six: Accountability   79

Chapter Seven: Follow Me   89

Chapter Eight: Go Ye   105

Chapter Nine: The Cross Factor   117

Chapter Ten: Transition is Empowering when Embraced   127

Chapter Eleven: Reject Not the Fathers   141

Chapter Twelve: Cost of the Double Portion   159

Chapter Thirteen: Let Integrity Guide You   173

Chapter Fourteen: God's Selection   183

Bibliography   193

PRELUDE

A very few of you may remember the book "God's Emerging Leadership" which I wrote in 1989. "An Incorruptible Heart" was initiated, as an updated version of that book, but it has developed with so much significant new material, which greatly increases the value and impact to the reader, that it has emerged as an entirely new book. These last 20 years have been fruitful yet stretching and have taught me much about understanding God's heart concerning leadership and those who desire it.

Many of you, of course, have never heard of "God's Emerging Leadership" let alone read it. So I continue these opening thoughts for you now. Some will initially pick up this book and wonder: "why the cartoons?" Initially, I must admit, it was simply because I like cartoons and thought the artist had done a great job. They say "a picture is worth a thousand words" and if that is so, then by their inclusion I have written a book hundreds of pages longer than this.

However, I also feel that they are a statement in themselves. Today we live in the era of the speed reader and those who can power themselves through a most impressive list of books each year. I have no criticism of that, however in that pursuit; I think it is possible that one can run the risk of beginning a book with a conquest in mind, rather than a contemplative hunger for God to speak deeply through the protective layers of the heart.

This is not a book to be read with speed. It is one to be thought upon, chewed over and taken in by one who desires the Holy Spirit to perform something eternal within us as only the Divine Surgeon can. We have included a reflection at the end of each chapter for this purpose.

The cartoons are to say "Selah". They are an invitation to pause and consider deeply the challenging truth they portray and the text about them. They are that waving of the arms that causes the driver of a freight train to grab for the brake and slow the momentum down.

My invitation to you is to join the ranks of those who have a deep-rooted cry for change and transformation and read these coming chapters as one committed to pleasing our Father. Pause often to listen to the Holy Spirit as He whispers His "Amen" to your heart.

INTRODUCTION

For the eyes of the Lord run to and fro in all the

whole earth to show Himself strong on behalf

of those whose heart is loyal to Him.

2 Chronicles 16:9

God is searching. He is searching for those in whom He can safely entrust the authority of His kingdom and the mantle of leadership within that kingdom. From the dawn of time God has searched for hearts that would not only leap in initial adoration of Him but, when desert winds had ripped at their faith and storms had lashed at their confidence, would still be found affectionate, loyal and trusting.

He has searched for those whose humility in the times of humble beginnings and relative obscurity, when subject to the acclaim of man and the applause of the crowd, would remain uncorrupted.

He has searched for those whose complete dependence upon Him in times of desperate need, when subjected to the beguiling influence of prosperity would retain the urgency of their cry.

He has searched for those whose kindness and generosity of spirit in times of poverty and lack, when subject to His abundance of supply, would pour out more not less.

It has been well said, *"power corrupts and absolute power corrupts absolutely"*. God has never lacked the zealous and the devout, the noble hearted warriors and the prophets with fearless gaze. He has never lacked the worshippers and the musicians with passion in their hearts and brilliance in their fingers and their song. What He has so tragically lacked is those who remain such when subject to the most dangerous of conflicts introduced to the human soul - success!

Success is not only vital for all those who claim to represent the Creator and His absolute rule, but considered by Him to be an essential quest for those seeking to truly honour Him. Success declares we serve a God that is able to empower and cause unreasonable achievement and excellence in the midst of a sea of mediocrity. Success declares that the wisdom He grants and the creative ideas He imparts are of greater value than experience or learning. Success causes the ordinary to achieve the extraordinary and the God that they serve worthy of awe and amazement. Success declares His greatness in the piece of clay He has chosen to mould and fashion.

Yet success also has within it, when not consecrated and submitted to divine control, the seeds of pride and self-advancement. In such cases its corruption of that which started out so pure, is merciless and thorough.

God's search today then, is for those whose attitudes and responses declare the presence of a grace-filled miracle, an incorruptible heart.

God is yearning to see His Church triumphant, the manifestation of His Son in His corporate body. For this to be a reality there must be the bestowing of His authority and dominion, not only in isolated places in Asia, Africa and South America, but in the Church of so called, affluent western nations. That is His challenge and His search to find a people whose hearts have remained loyal to Him in spite of success and the greatness of His provision.

In the pages of this book we examine what such people will look like. We peel back the layers of camouflage so skillfully protecting us from the trauma of seeing ourselves clearly in the mirror and talk openly about what the inner reality really looks like to the eyes of One searching for His Bride.

Chapter One
LOVE
or
LUST

Adolf Hitler:
A humble birth
A man of no physical prowess
A mere corporal in the German Army
A reject cast into prison
Yet:
He impacted his world
He left his mark on history
Why? What set him apart from other men?

General William Booth:
A humble birth
An upbringing of no consequence
Lived often in poverty
Attacked and ridiculed in the streets
Yet:
He impacted his world
He left his mark on history

Why? What set him apart from other men?

Hitler and Booth
Men with a difference
Men with a calling
Men with a destiny
What made them different from other men?
These men were leaders!
Born leaders
Compelling leaders
Powerful leaders

One excelled in his triumphs of evil, the other in his triumphs of good. Yet what they had in common was they were both destined to be leaders. The world has always had such people. People who have caused the happenings that others have merely read about.

They were the makers of history. We are its readers. They were the instruments of change. We are but those that live in its consequences.

Leaders are not ordinary people. They are the cutting edge. Those who open up for us the frontiers of tomorrow.

Leaders. Without them nothing moves, nothing happens. From the very beginning it has been so.

Adam's first commission was one that necessitated leadership as the Lord gave him his directive in Genesis 1:28 to "take dominion" over the works of His creation. As the Lord gave him the responsibility to name the animals in Genesis 2:19-20, it involved initiative and authority. The willingness to accept the responsibility of command.

> *"Out of the ground the Lord God formed every beast of the field and every bird of the air, and brought them to Adam to see what he would call them. And whatever Adam called each living creature, that was its name. So Adam gave names to all cattle, to the birds of the air, and to every beast of the field."*

It is then most obvious that God's intention was for people to be involved in the leadership of this planet. But what does one quick glance at history reveal?

Horror and trauma caused by the vain ambition unleashed via an outworking of that original pure and holy intention.

Did God make a mistake? Was man unfit for such a commission? Of course the answer is no!

History also records the many times when Godly leadership has arisen to save a nation, to restore a fear of the Lord. Many times when horror and trauma have, in fact, been averted because a man of leadership has taken the initiative and stood in the gap.

The question then is not one of leadership, or no leadership, but rather what kind of leadership,

Hitler and Booth. Two men with leadership calling. With each of them there was that moment of realisation. That moment when leadership desire became more than a passing whim. That moment when their acceptance of the call set their course and a leader was born.

It started with desire, the daydreaming of the heart.

Is such desire wrong? Is it presumptuous to want to lead, to touch a little of that which causes a person to impact their world?

It seems that Shakespeare thought it was so when he had Wolsey say:

> *"Cromwell, I charge thee, fling away ambitions. By that*
> *sin fell the angels; how can man then, the image of his*

Maker, hope to profit by it?"

Yet J. Oswald Sanders tells us that there are ambitions that are noble and worthy, and to be cherished and that scripture never warns against ambition itself but only against "self-centred ambition".

Sanders is right and here we discover a key. The desire for leadership in itself is neither good nor evil; its morality lies in the nature of its motivation.

In 1Timothy 3:1 (New English Bible), the Lord tells us that *"to aspire to leadership is an honourable thing"*. And yet in Jeremiah 45:5 he declares: *"Should you then seek great things for yourself? Seek them not."*

A person's motivation is critical! It is critical to the acceptance or rejection by God of what they seek to do.

If the motivation is pure, then God's acceptance of the actions will reflect it. If the motivation is selfish, then the resulting action will be void of pleasure to the Lord ... no matter how powerful that action might appear to be.

The desire to lead is therefore not in itself to be despised, but to be commended. However, it is the reason for that desire that should come under scrutiny.

Can it stand the test of Mark 10:42-45?

Jesus really came to serve; that wasn't a smokescreen for personal gain or profit. His motives were pure. His intentions genuine, unselfish, self-sacrificing.

"But Jesus called them to Himself and said to them, 'You know that those who are considered rulers over the Gentiles lord it over them, and their great ones exercise authority over them. Yet it shall not be so among you; but whoever desires to become great among you shall be your servant. And whoever of you desires to be first shall be slave of all. For even the Son of Man did not come to be served, but to serve, and give His life a ransom for many.'"

Be last, serve others – other focused by nature & motivation, not fronts for self.

Here the greatest leader of all time was revealing the true nature of

Paradigm shift - how do you value success & greatness ?

greatness. Servanthood and humility then becomes the measuring rod. They go hand in hand together.

In the beginning God created a leader. His name was Adam.

This leader was "in His (God's) own image" and reflected that image in his humanity. He was guileless and a man of humility. His benevolent dictatorship of this planet was a joy to his Father's heart. He ordered the animals; spoke for God, and peace ruled.

What promise this planet had and what a society such leadership could have produced.

But then came sin, the self-will of man. The dream was shattered and its potential lost.

Today we have a very different kind of world. Today our world is but the sad remains of God's intended Utopia.

"In the beginning God created a leader" It has been ravaged and plundered. Consecutive tyrants have come to whom the words of Jesus would have been irreconcilable with their own perverted view of what constitutes "Leadership of Strength".

World wars and global misery are simply the result of humanity's ambition for power and desire to rule rather than be ruled. Not that noble ambition of which Paul wrote, but the counterfeit of mankind's own selfishness and greed.

To see such mockery of the Genesis 1:28 statement in our Christ-rejecting world is sad indeed. However, of far greater grief to the Lord (and all those that love Him) is the alarming reality of how such pollution of His intentions has surfaced within the Church itself.

The very Body of Christ has suffered in like manner. The plunder mentioned has left the scars of mistrust and suspicion in countless thousands of individuals who are members of His Church. These casualties are in many cases, due to the wrongful use of power; a corrupted expression of the Divine mandate that the Lord initiated for the health and protection of those same members.

The tragedy is that when evil leaders rule, a universal principle of all leadership still applies - leaders reproduce after their own kind.

Many leaders today are producing a generation of young men and women to whom the pursuit of personal promotion and glory is considered an acceptable goal.

Is it any wonder then, that the Lord is currently laying a growing burden upon many to rediscover the true nature of that original mandate? He is also goading us to rediscover the character rules that govern its fruit in the lives of those who are impacted by it.

As mentioned previously, the vital area of concern is that of motivation.

Why? Because motivation is the source from which our priorities, philosophies and actions originate.

There are two basic motivations from which all others eventually emerge. These are 'LOVE' and 'LUST'.

The definition of these two is as follows:

LOVE:
- is for the benefit of others
- desires to give
- is at the expense of self

LUST:
- is for the benefit of self
- desires to get
- is at the expense of others

Ponder for a moment. Think through what you have just read.

What a challenge to:
- our reasons for marriage

- our reasons for business dealings
- our reasons for friendships
- our reasons for relationships
- our reasons for local church fellowship
- our reasons for leadership desire

What if we had to sit a test that applied this definition as a measuring rod to our motivations, attitudes and consequent actions? It is my contention that many of those in the leadership of the Church today would fail to pass with honour!

Paul warns of the extreme in Acts 20:29 as he states that after his departure from the church at Ephesus *"savage wolves will come in among you, not sparing the flock"*.

These "savage wolves" will not come with bared fangs plain for all to see, but will in fact come disguised as true men of God, raised up by Him as "His anointed".

The tragedy is that many will have started out as exactly that but have fallen prey to the lure of lust in one of its many and varied forms of enticement. The love of money, the love of public acclaim, the attraction of the eye toward the opposite sex, a desire to gather to one's self in order to protect from the insecurities of the future. So many have fallen in recent years.

A Contradiction

The Church of the 20th century has seen so much take place in the restoration of God's power and gifts. The Pentecostal and Charismatic movements have brought with them the gifts of prophecy, healings and miracles. There has been great release and deliverance and many testimonies of mighty deeds done in His Name. And yet, the contradictions also have been great.

Scandals have blazed their way across our newspapers and controversy across our screens. There has been:

- Financial empires of personal gain
- Countless Christian leaders caught in immorality
- War and rumours of wars between fellow Christians

Why? How can light and darkness run in harness together?

Such questions have led to many good people of God breaking away from the established church altogether in their disillusionment; the hillsides ring with the bleating of sheep that wander in dazed confusion.

For that reason alone we must bring enlightenment and scriptural comment on this subject of 'Motivation in Leadership'.

Matthew 7:15-23

> *"Beware of false prophets, who come to you in sheep's clothing, but inwardly they are ravenous wolves. You will know them by their fruits. Do men gather grapes from thornbushes or figs from thistles? Even so, every good tree bears good fruit, but a bad tree bears bad fruit. A good tree cannot bear bad fruit, nor can a bad tree bear good fruit. Every tree that does not bear good fruit is cut down and thrown into the fire. Therefore by their fruits you will know them.*

> *Not everyone who says to Me, 'Lord, Lord' will enter the kingdom of heaven, but he who does the will of My Father in heaven. Many will say to Me in that day, 'Lord, Lord, have we not prophesied in Your name, cast out demons in Your name, and done many wonders in Your name?' And then I will declare to them, I never knew you; depart from Me, you who practice lawlessness!"* (Lawlessness is of course the fruit of self-will.)

Jesus does not dispute that they have, in fact, done the deeds in question. He does, however, reject the reason for which they did them - their motivation.

Mark 13:22, 23

> *"For false christs and false prophets will arise and show signs and wonders to deceive, if possible, even the elect. But take heed; see, I have told you all things beforehand."*

Note it is not the signs and wonders that are false - it is the vessels through which they come!

Be an empty, clean, pure vessel for the Holy Spirit to pour into - He's the real deal, i'm just the vessel

2 Corinthians 11:12-15

> *"But what I do, I will also continue to do, that I may cut off the opportunity from those who desire an opportunity to be regarded just as we are in the things of which they boast. For such are false apostles, deceitful workers, transforming themselves into apostles of Christ. And no wonder! For Satan himself transforms himself into an angel of light. Therefore it is no great thing if his ministers also transform themselves into ministers of righteousness, whose end will be according to their works."*

Infiltration

I remember well an event in our local church not long after I had begun pastoring (Margaret and I planted a church at 25 years of age). We were young and vulnerable, small and eager to grow.

Then along came "Brother X".

What a man of apparent grace-so willing, so spontaneously encouraging. A man of great knowledge. He had apparently taught the Word in "Charismatic circles". How quickly he won peoples hearts! Yet deep within me, the Holy Spirit was screaming "Beware!"

I had nothing to hinge it on as his actions and words were beyond reproach.

But then it began.

People came to visit. They asked me when I would be giving him responsibility and the platform to preach, as he so obviously desired to minister more in that way. After all, the desire to minister is a noble one. But what was his motivation? Was carnal ambition at work or was this the Holy Spirit's doing?

I weighed it up.

The evidence so strongly seemed to affirm, but my stomach said "Yuk!" From within there was a resounding "No!" Yet many in the congregation were obviously expecting it.

I could tell that there would be tensions if God did not step in and I cried out for His intervention. I knew that He alone could orchestrate the necessary conditions for this man to show forth the true nature of his heart.

It is hard for me to remember exact details from that long ago, but for some reason the circumstances within the local church went through sufficient stormy moments to produce some strain in relationships generally.

In times like that the leader's credibility with people can go through a time of shaking and reappraisal. This in turn can indicate to those who are ambitious of heart, that this is their moment of destiny. It often takes a moment of controversy and shaking to reveal the true heart of a person.

One day it happened. The phone rang. A senior apostolic leader in our group of churches was on the line.

"Brother X" had arrived in his lounge and he had a list!

"The list" turned out to be accusations of my leadership and my character. To put it mildly, I was a fiend, an absolute dictator, a blot on the landscape of the Kingdom!

But that wasn't the worst. He had another list.

This list was all those in the church that supported the accusations and he had two thirds of the congregation on that list!

Now I really did feel ill. Scenes of me going back to selling furniture flashed before my eyes and I did what any other great man of God would do. Margaret and I headed for the beach!

For three days I walked that beach. I cried out for God's conviction – and got it!

God spoke to me about areas that needed adjustment. He spoke to me about areas He had been trying *"God could and did* to get my attention on. But none *speak into my heart"* of them were on "the list". On the items on that list I drew a complete blank. My conclusion was that the list was entirely unjust but if that was the way I was seen to be, then I would submit to whatever judgement was necessary.

We returned. Margaret and I pondered what the future might hold.

In our absence, the apostolic leader had done his homework and had spoken to all the "supporters" on the list.

They were amazed! Alarmed! Angry! None of them knew of the list. None of them supported the list.

Their words had been manipulated and misquoted. The whole affair had been the fabrication of that one tormented soul. When he was confronted he flew into a rage, manifested the abundance of his heart and needless to say, left!

The church came to a beautiful new oneness and love for each other and that particular intention of destruction came to nought.

On that occasion in our local church it was a happy ending, but on other occasions there has been heartache and tragedy. Occasions repeated many times throughout the Body of Christ.

So what was the point of it all?

Turn back to God before things get stupid

1. In the time of my desperate openness, God could and did speak into my heart. Subtle areas of motivation were adjusted. I discovered yet again, that provided we respond Godward rather than react manward, the Lord will always take that which the enemy means for evil and turn it for our good. The key is the humility of our response.

2. The circumstances of controversy were necessary to reveal the true heart of the wrongly motivated "Brother X".

In Numbers chapters 14-16, we see a parallel where the leadership of Moses comes under fire and the sons of Korah arise and endeavour to provoke a "coup".

They were leadership men; trusted men who had been in the ranks many years. The disloyalty and ambition of their hearts lay completely camouflaged until that moment when Moses seemed to have lost the support and understanding of the people. That was their time to strike – the time to manifest their hearts.

The result of course is tragic. Not only are they slain, but also those who *"offered up incense on their behalf"* die also – those who prayed for them and morally supported them without being part of the actual "coup" themselves. There are of course, degrees of such false motivation.

Don't drift - stay anchored to Jesus, nothing/no one else

There is the extreme of which Paul makes mention, and there are people who fit more into the category of those who have begun well but have been subtly enticed away. Either way, we have a contradiction between the motivation of the heart and the operation of the gift of God.

Don Basham puts it this way:

God's gifts - that He freely gives, they're not earned or deserved. Boast in Him when He gives, not in you who receives

"The gift says very little about the recipient (one receiving) but it does say a lot about the donor (the one giving the gift)."

He quotes 2 Corinthians 4:7

> *"But we have this treasure in earthen vessels, that the excellence of the power may be of God and not of us."*

He then states:

> *"What does the treasure represent? The wealth and riches of God. What does the treasure say about the earthen vessel? Nothing, except that the vessel holds the treasure. Such precious treasure in such humble vessels, Paul reflects, is a reminder that the power is God's and that we cannot make ourselves worthy of it."*

Don Basham's ongoing thoughts continue to stress the insignificance of the vessel and the paramount importance of the message and ministry flowing through that vessel. *Make sure vessel is clean & unobstructed so that the treasure can flow out to others. It's the treasure that is life-giving/changing*

He quotes Isaiah 50:10-11 about the Word not returning to God void and declares that:

> *"It is God's Word that shall prosper, not necessarily the one through whom the Word is ministered."*

So the message itself may still demand the affirmation of Heaven because of God's desire to reach mankind, but the person themself is entirely another question.

A person choosing to live in rejection of Christ's lordship can hardly be considered "His chosen vessel". Although God will always empower His Word to reach hungry people, the choice of the Lord to honour the individual can, and will be, reappraised according to the degree of that person's obedience and righteousness.

Let me quote the Psalmist in Psalm 18:20, 21

> *"The Lord rewarded me according to my righteousness; according to the cleanness of my hands he has recompensed me. For I have kept the ways of The Lord, and have not wickedly departed from my God."*

To be the "chosen of the Lord" is to know His sovereign hand of direction and as a result, experience His equally sovereign hand of protection. People who wilfully continue to live in defiance, are fools to expect that such a covenant remains intact regardless of the moral integrity of their lives.

Why? Because by their own freedom of choice, they have already broken (annulled) the covenant.

I cannot and do not say this with Pharisaic judgement, as I understand the responsibility that such judgement brings with it. I also (in compassion) must concur with Basham's observation:

> "A man with a powerful ministry is subject to far greater temptations than the average Christian. His position of unique privilege is also a position of unique peril!"

However, we must ask ourselves the question: How does such pollution of motivation take place? How can we recognise that such a peril is presenting itself?

REFLECTION

1. There have been many character casualties in the Church. In many cases due to the wrongful use of power – a corrupted expression of the Divine mandate. Have you seen this before? If so, what would you do differently in that situation?

2. Using the definitions of LOVE (for the benefit of others, desires to give even at the expense of self) and LUST (for the benefit of self, desires to get even at the expense of others), prayerfully examine each aspect of your leadership desire and expression and ask God if there should come any adjustment in attitude or action.

3. In what situations would you find your commitment to having a love motivation tested the most? What are the subtleties of those tests?

PRAYER

Father, I love you with all my heart but pause now to ask that at this time you examine my motivation in each area of life. I know that You love the Church more than I could imagine and that You are jealous over her. So without fear and without going on a witch-hunt but with a sincere heart I ask that if there is anything in me that is not pleasing to You, that You by Your grace and Your mercy will reveal it to me. If You show me something, I commit to dealing with it today.

Chapter Two

The JUDAS SPIRIT

Reminiscing over a cup of coffee, Bob looked over the table at his friend and thanked God for this friendship that had been such a wonderful part of his life for three decades. What a priceless gift Ken had been to him.

Bob was a highly successful church planter who not only had the largest church in his state but had planted some 100 churches over those three decades. Ken, of course, had been his "right-hand man" throughout this time and now was his closest friend.

With his children now all married, Bob told Ken that he had decided that he and his wife would take extended leave from the home church to travel around a number of their other church plants. He informed him that what released him to do so was his unqualified trust in Ken's loyalty and his giftedness to manage the church in his absence. The plan was to be away for nearly a year.

Ken was thrilled and they arranged to keep in touch almost daily concerning matters of the church. For almost six months Bob and Ken dialogued several times a week and not once was there a hint of concern.

Then Bob's son rang. Ken had been working in secret with some of the leaders and people undermining Bob's leadership and credibility. He had started his own church and taken over 300 of the people. As Bob and his wife wept at the tragic turn of events, they wondered how such a thing could happen.

It is a very good question. When does the heart of a close friend turn to become the betrayer?

Looking again at our definition of "love" and "lust" and to further understand the truth of that insight, I would like to examine the lives of three men in the scriptures. As we do this, we will see the moment when that peril presented itself and how subtly the enemy infiltrated the desires of these men.

Judas Iscariot

Judas was a close disciple and friend of Jesus for three and a half years. During this time he walked

> *"When does the heart of a close friend turn to become the betrayer?"*

the shores of Galilee with Him, he broke bread with Him, he suffered reproach with Him, he witnessed the miracles with Him and he sat down at supper-time to commune and fellowship with Him. He did this week after week, month after month, year after year. This was no surface relationship but rather one of depth and meaning. Yet this same friend and companion of the Saviour became His betrayer.

Why? How did Satan infiltrate this man's heart?

The answer, I believe, is revealed in Matthew 26:14-16.

> *"Then one of the twelve, called Judas Iscariot, went to the chief priests and said 'What are you willing to give me if I deliver Him to you?' And they counted out to him thirty pieces of silver. So from that time he sought opportunity to betray Him."*

From what time did he seek to betray him? From the time that he gave validity to the consideration *"What are you willing to give me if I deliver Him to you?"*

The true motivation of this man is suddenly apparent in that one statement. In other words, "regardless of the pain my decision will inflict upon another, I can stand to gain from this situation". Judas fell prey to the consideration of personal advantage at the expense of another. "What is in this for me?"

That's the Judas spirit!

21

Personal DESIRE vs. Someone else's WELLBEING.

Never underestimate it! That inner lust of the human soul to put one's own desire ahead of the wellbeing of others is a key component of the Adamic nature. It destroys relationship, corrupts noble goals and is a constant threat to God's intention in us all.

Gehazi

The same entrapment overtook this servant of Elisha in 2 Kings 5:20-27.

> *"But Gehazi the servant of Elisha the man of God, said "look my master has spared Naaman this Syrian, while not receiving from his hands what he brought; but as the LORD lives, I will run after him and I will take something from him."*

> *So Gehazi pursued Naaman. When Naaman saw him running after him, he got down from the chariot to meet him, and said, 'Is all well?' And he said 'All is well. My master has sent me, saying, 'Indeed, just now two young men of the sons of the prophets have come to me from the mountains of Ephraim. Please give them a talent of silver and two changes of garments.' So Naaman said, 'Please, take two talents.' And he urged him, and bound two talents of silver in two bags, with two changes of garments, and handed them to two of his servants; and they carried them on ahead of him. When he came to the citadel, he took them from their hand, and stored them away in the house; then he let the men go, and they departed. Now he went in and stood before his master. And Elisha said to him, 'Where did you go, Gehazi?' And he said, 'Your servant did not go anywhere.'*

> *Then he said to him, 'Did not my heart go with you when the man turned back from his chariot to meet*

> *you? Is it time to receive money and to receive clothing,*
> *olive groves and vineyards, sheep and oxen, male and*
> *female servants? Therefore the leprosy of Naaman shall*
> *cling to you and your descendants forever.' And he went*
> *out from his presence leprous, as white as snow."*

Gehazi could not understand why material gain had no appeal to the man of God. He reasoned that services rendered ought to be paid for and that if his master was not going to take advantage of the situation, then he most certainly would!

Here is where we must understand the incredible persuasive nature of human desire. It quickly gives way to self-deception and the ability to justify one's actions. In Gehazi's case there was room for quite logical reasoning that could have led him to ignoring the principles of honesty and integrity on this occasion. After all, was it not him that had come out to Naaman and delivered the message of healing and deliverance whilst Elisha had stayed within his own four walls? He could have reasoned that he had played as much part in the process of that healing as Elisha had and was therefore equally worthy of receiving some remuneration for the task.

> *"He allowed the desire*
> *for personal advantage*
> *to develop unchecked*
> *within his heart"*

His desire for personal gain gave way to dishonesty and self-deception, and although given the opportunity to regain the situation with the truth (verse 25), he chose not to do so.

The judgement of God came upon him in the form of leprosy and a vital and potentially great man of God was cancelled from the race. As the servant of Elisha he was next in line for the double portion principle. Elisha had served as the servant of Elijah and had received a double portion of his mantle and miracles. Gehazi would have, most probably, been in line for double the mantle of Elisha (four times the mantle of Elijah). What a tragedy that such a potential was never realised.

Why?

Because he allowed the desire for personal advantage to develop unchecked within his heart ... he echoed the words of Judas *"what will you give me?"*

Simon

Our third example is that of Simon the sorcerer whom we read about in Acts 8:9-13, 18-21.

> *"But there was a certain man called Simon, who previously practiced sorcery in the city and astonished the people of Samaria, claiming that he was someone great, to whom they all gave heed, from the least to the greatest, saying, 'This man is the great power of God.' And they heeded him because he had astonished them with his sorceries for a long time. But when they believed Philip as he preached the things concerning the kingdom of God, and the name of Jesus Christ, both men and women were baptized. Then Simon himself also believed; and when he was baptized he continued with Philip, and was amazed, seeing the miracles and signs which were done.*
>
> *Now when Simon saw that through the laying on of the apostles' hands the Holy Spirit was given, he offered them money, saying, 'give me this power also, that anyone on whom I lay hands may receive the Holy Spirit'. But Peter said to him, 'Your money perish with you, because you thought that the gift of God could be purchased with money! You have neither part nor portion in this matter, for your heart is not right in the sight of God.'"*

Simon was converted, baptized and followed in discipleship with Philip (verse 13). When he sees the tremendous authority and ministry respect that comes to Peter because of the gift function, his old desire for fame and recognition is resurrected. He offers them money to give him the gift with the words "give me" (verse 19).

Peter is quick to condemn this attitude and Simon is never heard of again.

Simon's character flaw was not love of money as with Judas and Gehazi, but rather the love of honour and recognition. Yet it was still an expression of the same root of lust: "Give me. What can I gain from this?"

None of these men could understand why financial gain and/or desire for fame had no appeal to the man of God. All three failed to perceive a most fundamental law of the Kingdom of God. Our service for the King must never be motivated by the desire for personal advantage.

With Judas and Gehazi it was for material gain, with Simon it was for recognition and respect. But with all of them it was the consideration of personal advantage.

Why do we get the corrupted preachers of this present age? What character flaw allows such unbridled self-serving to develop in the heart of one who may have started his race with genuine devotion? I believe that slowly but surely the desire for personal gain has been allowed to become entrenched as a valid consideration for many people. It was for very good reason that Paul said *"the love of money* (personal gain) *is the root of all evil"* (1 Timothy 6:10).

We must sound the warning to others who even now are being subtly infiltrated with this contamination of motivation.

- Prophets who prophesy for greater reputation and the acclaim of others.
- Preachers who preach to get bigger offerings (the introduction of the hireling mentality – going with the highest bidder).
- Givers that only give in order to get and to prosper.
- Servants who only serve in order to win favour and be exalted in due course.

With all of these, the motivation is selfish not selfless. They have lost sight of the cross! Laying down one's life for the sake of another.

"Somewhere along the line they stopped serving for the benefit of others"

Why are there ministers today, who once knew the blessing of the Lord, yet now are castaways with angry disillusioned hearts?

Why do people become bitter and resentful?

Somewhere along the line they stopped serving for the benefit of others and began to consider the possibility of personal advantage.

When that personal advantage was violated, they felt robbed or cheated and the sin of their own ambition opened their hearts to the curse of bitterness.

If only they had stopped to consider instead Philippians 2:1-22.

> *"Let nothing be done through selfish ambition or conceit."* (Verse 3)

> *"Let each of you look out not only for his own interest, but also for the   interests of others."* (Verse 4)

I remember all too vividly the alarm bells going off one day while talking with a pastor who had been in ministry for many years.

He had pastored this one group for much of his ministry and had given himself to the task. Then one day there was an unrealised expectation as his eldership denied him what they considered to be an unrealistic financial increase. The words he uttered that day later proved to be the beginning of the end: "But David, after all these years, they owe me something!"

It didn't sound unreasonable. He had served them for years. Perhaps the congregation's own appreciation was indeed lacking.

But something was fundamentally wrong. You see, if we have settled the issue of His ownership, His Lordship, then we also settle the fact that "we owe Him everything and He owes us absolutely nothing!"

It is you and I that will eternally be in debt to the Saviour of the cross. All that we do in service for Him is but our reasonable service (Romans 12:1, 2). It is not "martyrdom" or "fanatical dedication" or "sacrificial shepherding". It is our reasonable service!

But the Judas spirit sees all of life and ministry, not through the eyes of privilege, but through the eyes of self-interest. This degree of self-focus is of course, extremely unhealthy and leaves us vulnerable.

If we serve for our ministry's sake, we are vulnerable. If we serve to gain the admiration of people, we are vulnerable. If we serve to establish a base for our ongoing security, we are vulnerable.

Vulnerable to disappointment.

Vulnerable to hurt and wounding.

Vulnerable to resentment.

Vulnerable to hurting others as a result.

Why? Because we are vulnerable to the potential of unrealised expectation. But if we serve because of love for the King and His people, if we serve because of gratitude for the cross, if we serve because of appreciation of His awesome forgiveness and acceptance then such vulnerability is minimized. Our heart is shielded by an overwhelming sense of privilege.

This challenge comes to us all.

To some it is in the daily provocations of life and they are mercifully spared the "hour of crisis". I think, however, they are the rarity.

Disaster Strikes

Some years ago, the "big one" struck for Margaret and myself. It was a very swift slide down the hill from what had been considered as great success to absolute disaster; a stripping of finances, prestige, building, Christian school and of course, friends. My errors were not those of some great moral fall but errors of judgement. Decisions concerning leadership, decisions concerning the size of the building project, decisions concerning the amount of travel I was involved in at the time (travel and ministry that distanced me from my leaders and the congregation at a time when they needed the personal touch the most).

It was not a case of intentionally doing wrong but nevertheless making unwise judgements.

The whole glorious, furious pace of achievement had clouded my need to hear intimately from the King in matters of detail. Oh, the vision may have been His but as I have learned; the execution must also be His. *The vision and execution must be God's*

The consequences were swift in becoming apparent.

An offshore contract we had signed with a Bank turned out to be a disaster. We had signed over omnipotent powers to a small group of Foreign Exchange Advisors who proceeded to "buy and sell" on the International market using our money!

It was a nightmare. In a matter of months they took a $650,000 loan and produced a debt of over $1,000,000! Everyday the phone would ring with more and more bad news. I had our lawyer working to get us out of the contract but it was deemed impossible without paying back the original loan in its entirety. This we could not do as we had, of course, spent that money on the building project.

People started coming to the door wanting answers. Answers I did not have.

We finally began making those painful decisions that had become unavoidable. We had never failed to make a payment by its due date and we agreed that it would be dishonouring to the Lord to allow commitments to go unpaid. There was no alternative. We sold the property.

With the sale of the property, came the sale of the building so many had laboured on for many long months of sacrificial toil.

Our Christian school that had taken five years to build up also had to close. The parents were faced with the decision of what to do with the education of their children. This was the bitterest pill for me and many others. Oh how we loved that school and all those vibrant, wonderful kids.

Two homes on the property, one of them the house our own family were living in, also had to go. People were confused, bewildered and a number of them, understandably, simply left for less complicated waters.

How my heart ached for them. The pain I felt was not just for Margaret and myself, it was for them. Precious, beautiful people that I loved but now seemed so unable to protect from this awful reality.

As things deteriorated, it was necessary to stand before the congregation and ask their forgiveness for the hurt caused to many. I went to the Church that day dazed at how all this could be happening.

Then the gossip started. We learned afresh the power of discouraging and accusing words.

Some of those we had loved the most were those who wounded the deepest.

Some got "revelations" on how this was God-given judgement to purge the land from "false prophets".

Even one or two colleagues in the ministry took it as strong indication that God was annulling my call or at least the prophetic ministry.

Because of the controversy and questions, I stood aside from the leadership of a group of Pastors *"I thank God today that* that I had felt to gather together for *we clung to the cross"* prayer some years previous. Projects that we were doing together had to be rearranged so that I could melt away into the background. These leaders could not have been more personally loving and supportive but the steps were necessary if the events were to maximise their potential.

In the midst of this non-relenting barrage of discouragement, one of my leadership team shared that he felt to start up his own church down the road in Papakura.

I was shattered! This man was my friend, not just any member of my team. I had looked to him for support and encouragement. How could this be happening?

It became apparent that not only was this going to happen but that a large number of the people and some of the leadership had become persuaded to join him in the endeavour. After all, my own leadership appeared to be in tatters and an alternative at that time must have seemed incredibly appealing. My requests to postpone this process and to reconsider it after we were out of the crisis were not successful.

It is not for me to judge their heart in this matter as they sincerely felt that what they were doing was right, but it did not stop me feeling stunned and deeply wounded. I realised that this had enormous potential to bring contention should we declare our opposition to it and polarise people into taking sides on the issue. As the key person concerned could not be persuaded to reconsider, the only alternative was to publicly "bless" the new initiative and release people that wanted to go.

The weeping was done in private but in the pulpit I made it clear that there should be no negativity about this and that we wished them well. In my emotionally and spiritually depleted state, it was one of the hardest things I have ever had to do.

Our "dark night of the soul" had arrived. Margaret and I discovered in new depth the dealings of the Lord. We had to wrestle with forgiving those involved. We wept together and apart. Our life was becoming rubble and we cried out in our bewilderment.

In the midst of it we had many choices. But one choice stood out above all others.

Would we respond Godward or react manward?

Would we see the hand of God's allowance and run to the cross or would we fight for "our rights?"

I thank God today that we clung to the cross.

One day I silently cried out this prayer: "My God, what must I do to come out of this with my sanity intact?" His reply was so simple yet so incredibly powerful: "Keep your intimacy with Me and your integrity with people, and I will write the next chapter." That one phrase has been a guide to me, and the hundreds with whom I have shared it.

"Keep your intimacy with me and your integrity with people!"

Daily His grace became our sufficiency.

I realised that the 'He owes us nothing' statement was in fact a great and awesome truth. He has already given us everything in the person of His Son. If stripped naked but still accepted by His grace, we are immeasurably wealthy.

After the smoke had cleared and we had relocated, one part of the church to Manurewa and the other part to Papakura, we set about to see the Local Church re-established. When we deemed it strong enough, Margaret and I took the children to Seattle for three months to pour our souls out before the Lord. We had so many questions, so many hurtful memories, so many aching voids because of friendships ripped out of our lives. It took all the time we had allotted. But oh! How He met us.

He stripped us, He broke us, and He exposed those inner realities never faced before. It was so thorough until finally nothing seemed left but our love for Him. Forgiveness and genuine love filled our hearts toward those who had betrayed our friendship.

Then came the rebuilding, the resurrection, the fresh commissioning. What a gracious God we serve! How easy it is now to pour out our praise and adoration.

And it is in such times that we learn and discover keys of life for the benefit of others. As we now look back upon that season, we do not do so with hurt but with gratitude as we see the immeasurable wealth that God put inside of us at that time. Now, when ministering to pastors and leaders all over the world, we draw more from out of that "dark night of the soul" than from any other chapter of our lives.

What has my story to do with "the Judas spirit"?

It demonstrates that if we have kept our hearts free of such motivation, God will ultimately redeem even our weaknesses and errors of judgement.

The Judas spirit defiles the redemptive process; it corrupts the heart and hardens it against responding to God's correction and adjustment. Keeping a spirit of humility and maintaining a selfless love for God and His people allows God to refashion the broken vessel and restore them again to a place of honour.

REFLECTION

1. Our service for the King must never be motivated by the desire for personal advantage; whether that is love of <u>money</u>, the love of <u>honour and recognition</u> or the love of <u>anything else</u> <u>temporal</u>. What other things could be a negative motivation for serving the King?

2. What do you think of the statement 'God owes us nothing and we owe God everything'?

3. Have you been through a 'dark night of the soul' where everything was stripped away and you wondered if things could get much worse? <u>Were you aware of God's love and commitment</u> <u>to you in that time?</u> If not, have you walked through that with someone that has led you to that conviction?

4. In these times we can often have a 'martyr' mentality where we believe everyone else has done everything bad to us and we are without fault. <u>In your dark hour, did you ask God to</u> <u>reveal if there were areas in your life where you needed some</u> <u>element of adjustment or learn to do things a better way</u> <u>regardless of how others behaved? Were you able to do that</u> <u>with the confidence of God's unqualified acceptance that was</u> <u>not conditional upon the answers to that question?</u>

i don't want to waste my time trying to look perfect or have it all together. i don't. i'm not. Rather, God, help me to go deep with You, deal with my stuff. Really deal with it. So that i can be healed, i can be free. So that i can walk w/someone else & share - not a bunch of perfect wisdom or advice - but of my experiences with God & what He has done for me.

Freedom to not be perfect, to not have everything figured out, to just be me & discover who i am as i walk with Him.

PRAYER

Father I see how the subtlety of serving You and others with the motivation of personal gain can so easily creep in. I ask that You reveal to me if this is the case in my life. Father I am also aware that I have been through some very difficult times in life and that I have only done so because of your great faithfulness to me. I am so grateful for that. I am aware that You want me to learn how to become more like You and that these difficult times are opportunities for this to happen. This is not always easy Lord and right now I need Your strength. Lead me on Lord by Your grace, teach me Your ways and help me to respond towards You with a pure heart.

_____ *Chapter Three* _____

INTIMACY

Margaret and I have been married now for nearly 40 years. What started out as a romance soon went through the fires of challenge and contradiction which left us battle worn but determined to find the answers. This, by the grace of God, we have done and today have this deep and wonderful thing called intimacy.

Intimacy is not the romantic whim untried and protected from the storms that test it. Intimacy is a depth of love, devotion and commitment that deepens with the trial and remains unshakeable in the storm. It has been forged over time and can only be experienced by two people that selflessly give themselves to each other with abandonment and purity of motivation.

Intimacy is not fragile, it is robust and durable. Yet it does have that certain mystery, that awe at a love that seems inexhaustible and endless in its new horizons to be discovered. It is that overwhelming realisation that you both love and are loved so passionately and completely that it is impossible not to feel secure when with the object of such a love.

Intimacy is God's goal for His relationship with each of us. His is not the religious yearning for more members to be added to His Church. His is the cry of a Father that created us to live as sons and daughters and daily experience an intimacy with His heart that is both indescribably wonderful and unbelievably available.

He knows that such intimacy is the most powerful vaccine on Earth against the Judas Spirit. He knows that without it, even the most noble of hearts are fragile when exposed to the corrupting infiltration of success and man's acclaim.

I quote from an early writing of George Warnock:

> *"We do well to consider some of the dangers that lie in the pathway of the man who has authority from God, but who may be lacking in grace and mercy.*
>
> *Ministers who have power and authority vested in them by God are in a place of tremendous responsibility. For they may use the authority they have for good or evil, to fulfil the purposes of God or to justify or commend themselves.*
>
> *This is why it is so absolutely important that any minister exercising governmental authority comes into a higher relationship with God than that of his office … a relationship so intimate that he shall, in fact, minister out of the very heart of God Himself.*
>
> *Unless such a one pursues this goal, his very office could destroy him, as well as work havoc among the people of God."*

To avoid this, our place of safety as leaders, is in doing exactly what we would automatically counsel those in our congregations to do. Transparency with the Father, hunger for His presence, obedience to His daily directives, diligence in prayer and consistency in the study and application of His Word.

These are the source of one's true moral strength and fortitude and nowhere is it more vital than with those in leadership.

"Intimacy (with God) is the most powerful vaccine on Earth"

The contradiction represented in much of today's leadership (which we have already spoken of) is largely due to a subtle but definite eroding of this commitment in the lives of those "anointed". A commitment to intimacy with the King.

There are two kings of the Old Testament that so vividly portray this present reality to us.

Saul

Saul is most often referred to in a negative light. We fail to remember that much of what we see in his formative years we would recognise in the leadership of recent decades.

Take time out and read 1 Samuel chapters 9, 10, and 11 and note the following verses in particular. 1 Samuel 9:1-8, 16, 17; 10:6-13, 27 and 11:12, 13.

From these verses we see associated with Saul's early life some outstanding attributes.

1. Associated with power (1 Samuel 9:1) - *"a mighty man of power"*
2. Personal charisma (1 Samuel 9:2) - *"a choice and handsome young man"*

3. Tall of stature (1 Samuel 9:2) - *"from his shoulders upward he was taller than any of the people"* (head and shoulders above the people)

4. Determination and perseverance (1 Samuel 9:4) - *"So he passed through the mountains of Ephraim and through the land of Shalisha, but they did not find them. Then they passed through the land of Shaalim, and they were not there. Then he passed through the land of the Benjamites"*

5. Respect for God's anointed (1 Samuel 9:6) - *"and he (Saul) said to him... a man of God... he is an honourable man."*

6. Generosity (1 Samuel 9:8) - *"I have here at hand one fourth of a shekel of silver. I will give that to the man of God."* (Spoken by his servant but could only be carried out with his consent.)

7. Ministry of Deliverance (1 Samuel 9:16) - *"and you shall anoint him commander over my people Israel that he may save (deliver) My people from the hand of the Philistines"*

8. Strong authoritative leadership (1 Samuel 9:17) - *"this one shall reign over my people"*

9. Prophesy (1 Samuel 10:6, 10) - *"the Spirit of the Lord will come upon you and you shall prophesy, and he prophesied among them."*

10. Signs (1 Samuel 10:9) - *"and all those signs came to pass"*

11. Self-restraint and a controlled spirit (1 Samuel 10:27) - *"they despised him, and brought him no presents. But he held his peace"*

12. Mercy and forgiveness (1 Samuel 11:12, 13) - *"that we may put them to death." But Saul said, "Not a man shall be put to death this day"*

Who then was Saul a prophetic declaration of? The answer, I believe, is:

1. The anointing of a person's gift and office.
2. The yearning for power hidden within each of us in our inherited Adamic nature.

So often we associate Saul with his darker side that later came so much to the fore. We label him a scoundrel. We seem to forget that this mighty man of Israel was "the anointed of the Lord".

Samuel recognised him as such and so too did David. His initial ministry brought triumph and deliverance to God's people.

Saul was a man's man, a great warrior. A man that gave Israel the strong decisive leadership that it cried out for. In his formative years, Saul was a symbol of strength, of victory, of power; a charisma that had the people waving palm leaves. Triumphant, glorious, God-anointed days!

So much like the visitation of recent decades.

Since 1901 and the Azusa Street revival there has been many a power-filled ministry arise that has had signs, wonders and prophetic gifts. We have seen days filled with the miraculous, the excitement of joyous, new found horizons of faith.

There has been many a genuine visitation of the Lord to transform a near dying Church and catapult it into a 21st century demonstration of the book of Acts.

Since the turn of the last century, this great wind of restoration has progressively swept around our world and in many cases, brought harvest and a manifestation of God's power.

And yet, just as the nature of Saul was a mixture, so too has been the nature of this day of demonstration. Along with the power, we see the infiltration of those contradictions of character that have so marred the witness of this great move.

But why? Because, in Saul there was mixture; there was the presence of leaven. And so it is today with our own humanity. Along with the power and charisma of Saul, there was also self-will, ambition, desire for personal recognition and gain (i.e. the "Judas spirit")!

Samuel warned the people of Israel about this in 1 Samuel 8:10-18.

> *"This will be the behaviour of the king* (Pastor, Apostle or Leader of the Movement) *who will reign over you; He will take your sons and appoint them for his own chariots and to be his horsemen, and some will run before his chariot … will set some to plough his ground … he will take your menservants and your maidservants and your finest young men and your donkeys, and put them to his work. He will take a tenth of your sheep. And you will be his servants. And you will cry out in that day because of your king whom you have chosen for yourselves, and the Lord will not hear you in that day."*

Note the operative three words "he will take".

It was this element within Saul that he failed to effectively deal with and which eventually led to his defiance and disobedience of God's word to him via the prophet in 1 Samuel 13:9-14.

> *"So Saul said, 'Bring a burnt offering and peace offerings here to me.' And he offered the burnt offering... and Samuel said to Saul, 'You have done foolishly. You have not kept the commandment of the Lord your God, which He commanded you. For now the Lord would have established your kingdom over Israel forever. But your kingdom shall not continue. The Lord has sought for Himself a man after His own heart, and the Lord has commanded him to be commander over His people, because you have not kept what the Lord commanded you.'"*

"It takes time to know His voice"

When challenged by the prophet, we find there is no reference to any repentance or acceptance of guilt. His inability to receive correction with humility further developed the existing blind spot in his life and from this time on, things progressively deteriorated for Saul.

What can we learn from this tragic picture?

*His anointing was great, but it was an anointing bestowed upon him because of the necessity of his office (role) rather than the intimacy of his heartbeat with God.

He was not King because he was anointed; he was anointed because he was to be King.

*Saul underestimated the significance of true intimacy with his God and consequently neglected it as success was achieved. Doing the will of God in a general sense was for him sufficient. He failed to understand that only absolute obedience was and is acceptable obedience.

God is interested in detail as well as the big picture. He not only desires the right choice of canvas and brushes, He demands the right to apply the colour as and when He desires. The point is that this kind of obedience can only be a reality when one's ear is finely tuned to His voice and that takes intimacy!

I am not suggesting some legalistic enslavement to doing what God says out of fear of retribution.*My concept of true obedience is the fruit of love and devotion to a Father whose love for me is so overwhelming that it draws from me such a response. It is such a delight to know I have pleased Him and brought Him pleasure. Spending time with someone that loves you that much is not merely a discipline, it is an irresistible gravitational pull!

It takes time to know that voice.

It also at times, takes the wrestling of Gethsemane in order to understand (let alone obey) the details of His will.*There are times when what He knows in His wisdom is ultimately for our good and His purpose does not seem that way to us. Such times of enquiry and listening has to be given time.

Right now doesn't always equal good or God

Saul was too impatient for any such price. The glories of temporary triumph were within reach now! He was hungry for more conquest, more acclaim and more success. He wanted action now! After all, it could be reasoned that he was the "anointed of the Lord" and it was God's people that he was fighting for.

But this was a poor substitute for a holy and sovereign God who desired to fully possess Saul's heart, will and intentions. Jehovah wanted to be Lord then and He wants to be Lord today.

Now note 1 Samuel 16:1

> *"Then the Lord said to Samuel, 'How long will you mourn for Saul, seeing I have rejected him from reigning over Israel? Fill your horn with oil, and go; I am sending you to Jesse the Bethlehemite. For I have promised Myself a King among his sons.'"*

We can no longer continue to grieve for the inadequacies of a distorted Pentecost. We must cry out for the birthing of that fresh and totally pure move of God that is emerging even now in the hearts of those whose priorities and quest lie not in achievement, but in walking and talking with the Father in an intimacy both filled with awe, yet incredibly natural and spontaneous.

The contrast to this story of our "Pentecostal Saul" is, of course, that move of God that followed. The move that the Lord is bringing to birth in His Church right now that incorporates all that is powerful in Pentecost but has a new simplicity of heart!

David

David was not primarily anointed because of his office but rather because of his genuine love and desire to have an intimacy of relationship with his God.

*David, though also a great man of power, was first of all a worshipper and second, a shepherd! *Worshipper 1st, shepherd 2nd*

How does intimacy work with worship? It is to love and be loved and yet hold the object of that love in such awe and wonder that to sing His praises, is the spontaneous overflow of that love we feel inside.

Intimacy is not familiarity. It is not a lessening of the greatness of God and degree of privilege we should feel at being His son or daughter. Deep felt privilege does not diminish the value of the one feeling it. It merely indicates the degree of honour they give to the one they love. *To be both friend and servant is not only Biblical but also essential if we are not to reduce the dignity and beauty of our love to mere mortal attraction.

My Heavenly Father is my most intimate friend, yet He is the One of which David declares (and I echo) in Psalm 29:1-2:

> *"Ascribe to the LORD, O mighty ones, ascribe to the LORD glory and strength. Ascribe to the LORD the glory due his name; worship the LORD in the splendour*

of his holiness."

To "ascribe" is to declare and make known, to fully acknowledge, to proclaim, to cause all to know. For me to ascribe to Him greatness, awe and wonder, to acknowledge He is the Creator of Heaven and Earth and holds the Universe in the palm of His Hand, is not to place Him beyond reach. It simply floods my heart with gratitude and praise that such a One could so fervently and abundantly love one such as I. The sense of privilege I get from that is huge but the love and adoration it generates is indescribable!

Intimacy and worship, therefore, go together. One feeds upon the other, one stimulates and empowers the other. They are not a contradiction of terms but the most compatible of terms.

David was one that many times could have taken steps to further his own personal cause and gain, but chose not to because of integrity and obedience to the principles of the Lord - as in 1 Samuel 24:5, 6 when he spares Saul's life.

> *"Now it happened afterward that David's heart troubled him because he had cut Saul's robe. And he said to his men, 'The Lord forbid that I should do this thing to my master, the Lord's anointed, to stretch out my hand against him, seeing he is the anointed of the Lord.'"*

David was more convicted about cutting the hem of Saul's garment, than Saul was about throwing a javelin at David! How different the hearts of these two men were.

It has been my privilege to know some "Davids". Men and women with such purity of spirit - guileless men and women, with no thoughts of furthering their own cause. Their devotion to their God is clearly seen in their unswerving devotion to others, whether they are worthy of it or not.

The difference between the two men was that:

- Saul was anointed because of his prowess
- David was anointed because God saw him as a man after His own heart

Today, power and authority are once again mixed with leaven. In many cases, the reign of Saul is established and men and women of stature rule over God's people.

What's really the goal - anointing: personal recognition OR rel. + intimacy w/God?

Anointed, gifted, empowered; but not necessarily because they know God more intimately. Many are anointed for no other reason than they have an office and a calling. Great are their public victories, yet great are their personal inconsistencies, and as a result, we see again and again the tragedy of their collapse.

Who has not been grieved over the fall of some great man or woman and wondered how one so mightily used of God could have ended up so tragically?

Let me quote you from 2 Samuel 1:19, 21 & 25 (concerning the death of Saul):

> *"the beauty of Israel is slain upon the high places; how are the mighty fallen ... the shield of Saul, as though he had not been anointed with oil ... how are the mighty fallen in the midst of the battle!"*

What an anguished cry! But why do we wonder at it?

Because we fail to realise the potential that lies dormant in the old nature of the human heart. A potential that is bolstered and energised every time our personal will prevails when challenged by the will of the Lord's intention. It is then that an unholy conception takes place and the serpent of pride and self-indulgence brings forth after its own kind once again.

James 1:15, 16

> "When lust (desire to please self) has conceived, it brings forth sin; and sin, when it is finished, brings forth death"

And Saul, who had slain his thousands in conquest for God, died by suicide after having first backslidden to the point where he dabbled in the occult. Friends, all because of self-will, independence and pride. What an underestimated foe our self-will really is!

So subtle yet so powerful are desires never surrendered.

If we were to be honest, we have all known times when, if we saw things through His eyes, we would see in ourselves ambitions never nailed to the cross, personal goals never submitted to His Lordship and areas of "no trespass" to the Holy Spirit.

It is not that we consciously rebel. We simply do not consciously and intentionally submit. Independence brings with it a false sense of ones own capacity to cope, that sees no need of submitting plans to the scrutiny of another.

The more apparent success we achieve, the more vulnerable we become. Some of the most dynamic of ministries have revealed the greatest of flaws.

When talking of contradictions over the last century, Bob Mumford said that such men and women fall into the trap of *"confusing the Creator with the created"*.

In other words, they begin to feel that the power-gift is now theirs. They are anointed because they deserve it and they can initiate what they wish and "the power" will always be at their disposal.

They lose more and more, their sense of dependence on God's directives and a reliance on the person of the Holy Spirit. They lose sight of the reality that they

> *"they confuse the Creator with the created"*
> *- Bob Mumford*

minister simply by His grace (His unmerited and undeserved favour). Such men and women inevitably stray from God's original intention as they become increasingly unable to hear His voice clearly. The result is acts of disobedience.

I have become increasingly convinced that there is a grave need to freshly establish our theology on the person of the Holy Spirit. He alone is the source of God's supernatural demonstration on the earth and we must not fall into the trap of divorcing Him from carrying out His purpose.

The term "anointing" has not always been used biblically, and in some cases, is referred to as something additional or apart from the actual person of the Holy Spirit. This then opens the door to a progression of thought that allows one to use the "anointing" regardless of ones relationship with the Person. Consequently, one can, with this theology, allow for the living of a life incompatible with the Person yet still moving in the "anointing". I find in this an explanation of how it is that people living immoral, greedy or selfishly ambitious lives, can still offer God's people the entertainment of various demonstrations and claim them as evidence of that "anointing".

Reference to the "anointing" is proper and valid, but only as an extension of the Person. When we say that "there is an anointing present to prophesy", we are saying that it is on the Holy Spirit's agenda to prophesy in that meeting. When we say that "there is an anointing present to heal", we are saying that it is on the Holy Spirit's agenda to heal in that meeting.

If we are to stay pure of heart and compatible with God's heartbeat, we must never divorce His acts from His Person. The consequence of doing so is to start down the path of independence that calloused Saul's heart from hearing God clearly and responding fully.

However, it must be stressed that the above will never be an issue for the one who has discovered and daily lives in true intimacy with the Father's heart. When one is hopelessly addicted to loving Him, listening to Him, yearning to please Him, one is assured of being under His directorship. What a boldness and courage that brings!

REFLECTION

1. How well do you recognise God's voice? How often do you hear God's voice?

2. When you hear God speak, do you obey quickly and fully, or are there circumstances in which you find that more difficult?

3. Do you find it easier to worship than to exercise your gift?

4. The problem is not that we consciously rebel but that we don't consciously submit. Are there areas of your life and ministry that you have not consciously submitted to God?

5. Obedience is more acceptable to God than sacrifice. Are there areas of your life in which you are offering God a sacrifice (your work or service) to compensate for a lack of obedience in another area? We have all done that at some stage but be encouraged to take a moment of honest reflection and, if necessary, bring that issue to a new place of full surrender.

PRAYER

Father I know that intimacy with You has got to be number one in my life. If I am honest I also know that this is often the first thing to go when I get busy and have deadlines. I need to change this Lord and I make a commitment today to be consistent in my times with You. I would also commit myself to a greater level of full obedience. I know that some of the things that You ask me to do are difficult and sometimes they don't even make sense, but I also know that I trust You and You know best. Lord I submit to You today.

_____ *Chapter Four* _____

INFLUENCE WITH GRACE

Saul was mighty in the anointing, mighty in prophesy, mighty in battle; but because he "spared Agag and the best of the sheep" it brought him to ruin. The fact that he would dedicate these to the Lord made no difference. Obedience was God's intention, not sacrifice.

*So often we take the fruit of our own self-will and in dedicating it to God, ask Him to bless it. It doesn't work!

It wasn't acceptable then, and it isn't acceptable now.

Now, let us consider one further warning.

In 1 Samuel 13:13, 14 the kingdom is taken from Saul.

> *"And Samuel said to Saul, 'You have done foolishly. You*

> have not kept the commandment of the Lord your God,
> which He commanded you. For now the Lord would
> have established your kingdom over Israel forever. But
> now your kingdom shall not continue. *The Lord has*
> *sought for Himself a man after His own heart*, and
> the Lord has commanded him to be commander over
> His people, because you have not kept what the Lord
> commanded you'."

And yet in 1 Samuel 14:47 (one chapter later) we read *"Saul established his sovereignty over Israel"*.

How can this be? The crucial word is "his".

He established his sovereignty (his control).

Now no longer able to lead by the anointing, his human reflex is that of every man in his position since. He increased structure and control to compensate for his lack of anointing.

This is, of course, the history of denominationalism where those in leadership of a movement do likewise. The need to retain the loyalty and commitment of members becomes more and more desperate, as one subconsciously is aware that such factors are on the wane.

At this point we face the choice. Respond Godward, or react manward.

You can either go to your knees before the Cross, or you can allow manipulation and control to motivate ever-increasing degrees of structure and law.

Once again, the subtlety of this thing is its peril. We see it also in the context of a local church. No genuine leader sets out to become a manipulator. However, with the pressure of people leaving or threatening to leave, it is so easy for him to begin to automatically see such happenings as "manifestations of the flesh" or "attacks of the devil". He sees the murmurings of the sheep as a sign of this present lawless age and vows to combat it with some good "black and white

There is indeed a work of the devil and the flesh involved, but not as he supposes.

True, much of the original complaints may have been petty and self-serving. True, the members of the congregation involved need a renewed vision of the cross and the Lordship of Christ. True, they are supposed to submit to their God-given leadership. And yes, true, they will have to one day answer to a holy God for their part in this rending of His Body.

But what of the leader's part? With every determined blast the gap between the leader and the congregation grows wider. With every thunderous reminder of the legality of the law, the leader compounds the congregation's concept of the leader as one who no longer cares for them with a selfless shepherd's heart.

And then there are the politicians. They are the leaders who would never dream of such openly inappropriate expressions of self-rule.

These are those who skilfully manipulate the hearts and relationships of God's people in order to achieve their own agenda. Their approach to conflict is not to seek God but to ensure their own survival in leadership. To them success is not the development and release of people but that they have played the game in such a way that brings them maximum recognition in a personal benefit.

Whereas the public displays of arrogance and control are ugly, the well disguised manipulations of God's people are sinister and just as deadly.

Because the leader fails to see the need for their own personal and individual brokenness before God, they allow the conflict to produce an ever-increasing insensitivity toward the congregation and toward the voice of the Lord.

Quoting George Warnock:

> *"Some of God's shepherds have been slow to understand the heartache and the agony of God's sheep in times of spiritual drought and apostasy. And when God begins to call the sheep unto Himself and into union with Himself alone, and they begin to depart from established church systems and structures, there is usually consternation and dismay among the leadership. And very often this brings about a tightening of the strings of leadership in order to coerce the sheep into obedience to their authority."*

> *"The fact of the matter is that sheep, God's sheep, are longing for true guidance and true leadership _ but their hearts grow weary and their souls become dry and thirsty as they go from one pasture to another looking for true rest"*

Now, I know that in including such a quotation I run the risk of being misinterpreted. Let me emphasise here that he is not justifying "gypsy saints" who wander about year after year without a fixed abode or

Christians who do not submit to authority because of their pride. The Bible is clear that we must be established in a local Church in order to grow into a well-balanced disciple. It is not those who are found in the house of the Lord that grow; it is those that are planted! (Psalm 92:13)

Godly oversight is vital and submission to that oversight is a scriptural command. Providing, of course, that that overseer is a lover of God.

Warnock was not talking about the "Davids"; he was talking about the "Sauls".

Men and women who no longer serve, no longer pray, no longer walk in intimacy with the King.

Arrogant and unteachable people. Sauls.

Controlling, manipulating and yet blind to it all. Why? Because they still appear to be able to get results; they still lay claim to manifestations of the "anointing".

Poor Saul, he retains the outward resemblance of being in authority, but the God-essence was gone.

What a pathetic picture.

Not that his anointing was gone (we've all had moments of that), but that he was so totally unable to discern it.

No wonder he fell on the field of battle.

It takes the moment of crisis so often to reveal the true nature of our state. All can appear as normal until that temptation or contradiction suddenly presents itself.

Then, like the hollow shell that we have become, we collapse!

Saul lost the battle with self-will long before he lost the battle with the Philistines.

We have a parallel to this in the life of Samson where his compromise in the moral area gives his adversary the opening to defeat him.

Judges 16:19, 20

> *"Then she lulled him to sleep on her knees, and called for a man and had him shave off the seven locks of his head. Then she began to torment him, and his strength left him. And she said, "The Philistines are upon you, Samson!"*
>
> *So he awoke from his sleep, and said, "I will go out as before, at other times, and shake myself free!" But he did not know that the Lord had departed from him."*

The tragedy is that, *"he did not know that God had departed from him"* - again, defeat is the result.

The waning of his intimacy with Jehovah had been such a subtle thing. Just a little each day. Allowing the weeks to go by without arresting the situation.

So vulnerable to a decrease in moral vigilance.

So vulnerable to thinking that just a little lowering of the standards wouldn't hurt. After all, when weighed up against his glorious endeavours it was such a small thing to begin with.

Small things grow.

Compromise always grows.

Samson had lost his hatred of evil.

Men and women of intimacy do not think that way.

People of intimacy know that their love for righteousness must be a passionate fire. A fire to be fuelled in His presence daily. They know that without His sustenance, His sufficiency, His grace - they are vulnerable.

The God-essence must be there and His life must flow in them.

For Samson this was no longer a reality.

But it took a moment of crisis to find it out.

And crisis is always too late.

We see the same principle in Matthew 23:38, 39 & 24:1 where Jesus says to the Pharisees ...

> *"'See! Your house is left to you desolate...' Then Jesus went out and departed from the temple."*

The absence of Jesus causes the temple to become desolate and yet nothing outwardly changes. For year after year, the priests held their services just the same and no doubt many would have mocked those words of Jesus.

The songs were the same. The programmes were the same. Somewhat predictable, but all still there.

But! Then came the Roman legions to destroy and plunder.

The living church of the risen Christ is warned by prophecy and escapes in its entirety.

The temple, however, is ransacked and its priests shattered in humiliation.

They were desolate.

But, if only they had known it, their greater desolation was not the cruelty of the invader but the exit of the Messiah they had chosen to reject.

Like Saul, they had lost the kingdom.

What does it mean, to "lose the Kingdom"?

It means that the God-essence is gone.

His presence has departed.

As a result, it means that one's dominion (God-given authority to rule) has also departed.

Many a Saul today may have retained the human power to subject others or to exercise some gift, but that in itself is not evidence of "The Kingdom".

The Kingdom (Rulership) of God is that which can stand the test of having dominion in the realm of spiritual realities.

It is that anointing born of intimacy with His heart.

It is that reflection of His character that is unassailable in its integrity.

It is that sovereign touch of the Divine that inflames our hearts and demands the response of those to whom we minister.

*The Kingdom is spiritual reality that declares God's rule is established in that environment.

When the Kingdom is present, we don't have to "work it up" with hype! Its awesome outworking is but the natural expression of having the King in His triumphant Lordship in our hearts.

Today is often the day of the 'Evangelist extraordinaire'. The song leader that is part entertainer and part gymnast.

They really know how to have the people in full roar. The wilder the beat and the more frenzied the dance, the greater the success. Emotions run high and a "wow" of a time is had by all.

Not that fervent celebration in itself is wrong. In fact, we should rejoice at such times. But is it necessarily the emotion and volume that indicate spiritual reality and the level of ones spiritual authority? I don't think so.

*The declaration to the forces of darkness that we have the right to rule is not the eloquence of our rhetoric, nor the enthusiasm of our antics.

It is simply that we have the sceptre in our hands.

According to Hebrews 1:8-9 the sceptre of God's Kingdom is *"a sceptre of righteousness"*. The sceptre is a declaration of inner purity - both in internal attitude and motivation as well as in lifestyle that allows the authority of God to be expressed through us.

That same scripture tells us that Jesus was *"anointed more than His fellows ... because he loved righteousness and hated iniquity"*.

It is not in what He did, but rather in who He was. So it is true today. True success is who we are in God, not in what we do for God.

The life that accomplishes a work eternal is neither necessarily loud nor necessarily soft. It is not in style or in degree of training. It is simply His life. His life that is able to flow through a totally submitted vessel.

Structure or Not

For Saul, structure was his means of control. His manipulation depended on it.

Does that mean that one's motivation and true anointing can be seen in the degree of structure that one requests?

No, not at all.

My own conclusion is that it is not a matter primarily of authority or not, structure or not, programmes or not; but rather, whether one ministers with the heart of a Saul or that of a David. It is whether his confidence is in the fact of his office alone or in his intimacy with and dependence upon the Lord.

Sauls will always gravitate towards self-motivated control. Davids will always gravitate towards loving God's people with a grace filled heart, sensitive not only to God's voice but also to those they have influence with.

REFLECTION

1. 1. Do you believe that the vast majority of people will love those who consistently love them? If so, how should this affect the initiatives we take when communicating with people?

2. In what ways can a parent or a leader allow the pressures of bad attitudes in others to draw them towards those subtle degrees of manipulation or control?

3. Psalms 37:4 tells us to "delight in the Lord". In making oneself busy in the work of the Kingdom, it's important to maintain that sense of "delight". How often to you take time out to "delight in the Lord"? How does it affect those you serve when you do? Or when you don't?

PRAYER

Father, I know the greatness of your love for me and I marvel at it. I know that it is impregnable no matter how I respond at times because you know my heart. Help me to see others through your eyes and to allow them the same sense of security in the love that I have for them. In Jesus Name, Amen.

Chapter Five
SERVANTHOOD

They walked into our lives one day in 1979. They were tall, elegant and gracious – their gentleness of spirit verging on timidity. The one thing that was established very early was that public platform ministry was definitely not their strength. In fact, the thought of it would bring on a mild case of blind panic!

So soft and compassionate. Obviously decisions demanding a degree of firmness and objectivity would be most difficult. Decisions of correction and judgement almost impossible. And yet it happened and the unbelievable came true.

Today they Pastor a successful, growing Church. They both have a wonderful ability in public. Their sermons are empowered, anointed and filled with truth that impacts your soul. He serves on the National

Executive of their Movement and has enormous credibility throughout the nation and overseas.

They govern wisely. <u>Difficult decisions are made with Godly objectivity and always with scriptural integrity</u>. We look on and we praise God for it all.

But why? Why did God choose them to reveal His awesome wonder in such a manner?

They were servants.

In <u>motivation</u>, in <u>attitude</u>, in <u>action</u>, <u>they were servants</u>. We watched as God anointed increasingly and more responsibility was given. <u>Their servant hearts remained</u>. — *the constant*

We watched when things got rough. I mean, very, very rough. My own authority was reeling under wave after wave of criticism and attack.

Some thought they should have taken the Church then. We watched.

True, honourable servants. <u>Their integrity never wavered</u>. Today they have recognition and authority. Their ministry has produced a strong missionary-minded local church. They have respect from all who know them.

But what has this done to their servanthood? Nothing.

* You see, <u>true servants have no appetite for personal glory</u>. <u>They live in eternal appreciation</u>. <u>A sense of deep privilege fills their hearts</u>.

<u>Servants they were, servants they are</u>. God knows He can trust <u>such with His Kingdom</u>.

Thank you Lord for examples like Jim and Anneke!

Frank Damazio states:

> *"Most people understand a leader to be one that directs, administrates, organizes, makes decisions, delegates responsibilities, and makes plans for the future. This*

definition, however, lacks a very essential part of what it means to be a true leader: one who serves. A leader of God's people must have the inner attitudes, motivations, and outer service of a servant."

Frank has summed it up well. The outer service is only as acceptable to God as the reality of the inner attitude and motivation. In this time of examining motives, there can be no more vital subject to consider (other than one's intimacy with the Lord) than this thought of servanthood.

It is in the heart of a true servant that we discover the beauty of humility and meekness; strength under control; the selflessness expressed in the joy of serving another without the thought of personal benefit.

Servanthood is that quality that Paul wrote of when he exhorted the saints at Philippi (Philippians 2:5) with the words:

> *"Let this mind (attitude) be in you."*

He leaves us in no doubt as to the definition of servanthood in verses 3 & 4:

> *"Let nothing be done through selfish ambition or conceit, but in lowliness of mind let each esteem others better than himself."*

> *"Let each of you look out not only for his own interests, but also for the interests of others."*

In verses 20 & 22 he describes Timothy as one who will "sincerely care for your state" and that he has seen solid evidence of this in the life of Timothy as he "served with me in the gospel."

Peter G. Wiwcharuck has stated that motivation may be either:

> *"an internal force which drives the human being to greater achievement or an external force ... such as social pressures or the whip of a task master"*

The nature of true servanthood is that it is entirely voluntary and comes out of one's desire to please the Lord and be of value to another. Servanthood does not, therefore, have as its conscious goal the acclamation of others nor the promotion that it might bring. Such objectives don't do away with the value of the acts of serving, but certainly do cancel the eternal value of the motivation being expressed.

Paul was obviously aware of this potential to complicate one's reasons for that which they do.

In Philippians 2:12 he exhorts them to act in obedience "not as in my presence only, but now much more in my absence". What Paul was saying was that he knew full well how they could act when he was around to see it and to be impressed by it, but how would they act when he was not there and when there would be no promotional benefit coming from the recognition of those acts?

Now, I had better pause here and make a point. Being required to serve with zeal and commitment is a vital aspect of character development in anyone being trained for ongoing responsibility and leadership, whether it is voluntary or not.

It may well be anything but voluntary to begin with, but nevertheless must be seen as an inescapable demand for those aspiring to one day exact that servanthood from others.

However, though essential with either attitude, it is only as it flows freely from the heart of one who is doing it voluntarily that it is seen by God as evidence of Christ-likeness. This Christ-likeness is what He is looking for when issuing a commission of increased authority.

It is the very absence of such motivation that withholds the hand of God so often when He otherwise would have further commissioned a particular vessel.

And yet so many of those given the responsibility of training and releasing others into leadership choose to ignore the seriousness of this requirement. It has been well said that "prevention is better than cure" and much of the tragedy caused by impurely motivated leaders today, could have been avoided with greater diligence being applied in the initial stages of their training and development.

In 1 Corinthians 4:2 (NIV) Paul declares:

> *"It is required that those who have been given a trust must prove faithful."*

Servanthood and faithfulness, of course, go hand in hand. Faithfulness is the very essence of servanthood. In 2 Timothy 2:2 Paul again instructs regarding the choice of those to take leadership and tells Timothy *"commit to faithful men"*.

But who do we choose today? Who is it that catches the eye the quickest? So often it is the one with charisma, the one with talent, the one with energy, the one with gifting.

All of which are great attributes. But, without servanthood they could have excellence and still end up a Saul.

"Faithful: one whose dependability is such that you can form a faith conviction concerning it"

In 3 John 5 we have the exhortation *"Beloved, you do faithfully, whatever you do"*. Note the word "whatever".

Faithfulness (servanthood) is never dependent upon what we consider to be our ministry or calling. It is an element of Christian character!

This character is essential to us all and to be evidenced in every task given into our charge. Nowhere is it more essential than in the developing lives of those that one day are to take the awesome responsibility for human lives in the Kingdom of God.

Joshua was a great example of this. We know Joshua as the mighty warrior, as the great leader, as the successful heir to Moses who took the Children of Israel into the Promised Land. Here was a man of awesome authority, great miracles and a very sizeable congregation indeed!

And yet, this Joshua was not picked for such responsibility lightly. God had had His eye on him for some time. Under the scrutiny of Jehovah's all-seeing eye, this man had proven vital qualities over and over again. He had not only proven that his devotion to God Himself was unwavering and worthy of trust, but also that his loyalty and faithfulness to the one that God appointed over him, was just as worthy.

Frank Damazio speaks concerning the servanthood of Joshua:

> "Joshua was known in Israel as Moses' minister or Moses' servant. The 'servant of Moses' was his official title. He was never called the 'servant of Jehovah' until the Book of Joshua, after Israel had entered Canaan. The words 'to minister,' used in the Book of Numbers and the Old Testament concerning Joshua meant 'to attend as a menial worshipper, to contribute, to serve another, to wait on others.' The word for servant in Exodus 24:13 'Moses and his servant Joshua,' would be equivalent to the New Testament Greek word 'diakonea', or deacon. Joshua was willing to serve Moses and to be known as Moses' deacon. The leadership principle found here in the life of Joshua is for a leader to be faithful to others as servant, then afterwards, realise that God will use him as His servant."

So what does this word "faithful" actually mean?

The word "faithful" when applied to the lifestyle of an individual literally means: one whose dependability is such that you can form a faith conviction concerning it. A person predictable in their consistency, in their devotion, in the purity of their motivation.

Paul spoke of Timothy this way in Philippians 2:19-22

> "But I trust in the Lord Jesus to send Timothy to you shortly, that I also may be encouraged when I know your state. For I have no one like-minded, who will

sincerely care for your state. <u>For all seek their own,</u>
<u>not the things which are of Christ Jesus</u>. But you know
his proven character, that as a son with his father he
served with me in the gospel."

"Sincerely", "faithfully," with predictable commitment.

Paul was saying that Timothy was a man in whom he could safely trust! He didn't have to be concerned about his motivation or his dependability.

Timothy was the kind of man you could count on. And how had he proved this? By his serving!

Not by his eloquence, not by his gift manifestations, not by his charisma, but by his willingness to serve.

The tragic note in this scripture is when Paul declares:

"I have no one other than he"

But Paul? What about all the young men, the disciples that chose to come and sit at your feet? No one!

"Oh, I could get volunteers to preach, to song lead, to carry the banner at the front of the parade. But those who will faithfully (sincerely) 'care for your state,' that's different!"

72

Why? Because now we are talking of servanthood, now we are talking about selflessness.

Now we are talking about verses 5-7:

> *"Let this mind be in you which was also in Christ Jesus, who being in the form of God, did not consider it robbery to be equal with God, but made Himself of no reputation, taking the form of a servant, and coming in the likeness of men."*

And that cuts out the majority in the Church today, just as it did in Paul's day.

I can now look back over 42 years of watching fiery young zealots being born. So many with so much potential.

Many of these were gifted, talented, and extremely able. The whole world awaited their life and ministry. Yet so very few can be found today still fulfilling the Master's call. Just the servants remain, or those that God has graciously broken to become such.

In the Old Testament, this was the kind of a man that Kings would look for when trying to find an armour bearer. No man had greater responsibility in the time of battle; the very life of the King in fact depended upon it. Obviously loyalty was a key thing the King would look for, but loyalty alone was never enough. There had to be more than that.

The King had to know the man's diligence, his vigilance and his sense of discipline. These things were beyond question. They were predictable!

A person might genuinely love you and in their heart consider themself to be loyal to you, but if they are not dependable, then they are useless in the time of battle!

You can retain them as a friend but don't give them the responsibility of human life.

Why? Because we are at war. We are involved in the greatest battle, the greatest conflict this world has ever seen. The battle for the souls of people!

A Pattern of Behaviour

How would a King discover such qualities?

The same way Paul did.

He would observe the person over a period of months or years in various menial tasks in order to establish a pattern of behaviour.

Paul knew that a person's attitude toward the greater responsibility would be exactly what they had demonstrated toward the lesser responsibility.

He knew that a person's character does not change because of function – that is a lie!

- What they are with a new convert, they will be with a Home Group.
- What they are with a Home Group, they will be as an Elder.
- What they are as an Elder, they will be as a Pastor.
- What they are putting out the chairs, they will be with the Community Ministry.
- What they are with the Community Ministry, they will be as a Deacon.
- What they are as a Deacon, they will be as the Church Administrator.

One must always look at the track record.

Believing for change, anticipating change, but never rewarding it before it becomes a reality!

The work of the Kingdom is too precious! Human life is too precious!

Luke 16:10

> *"He who is faithful in what is least is faithful also in much; and he who is not faithful in what is least is not faithful also in that which is much."*

It's a law!

Today there are all too many who seem to think that God has forgotten that He ever established this principle; that somehow it is to be different for them. They feel they have the right to pick and choose their faithfulness and their consistency in things that they have previously committed themselves to attend, but now find too mundane or sacrificial.

"A person's character doesn't change with their function"

And yet they will still expect God to take their word for it when they tell Him that they will be faithful if given the opportunity for a touch of recognition and glory.

They quote the fact that "so-and-so" didn't have to prove themselves; they apparently just "shot to the top".

Let's take a look at Proverbs 20:21:

> *"An inheritance gained hastily at the beginning ... will not be blessed at the end."*

In recent years we have seen an alarming new trend in placing relatively new young Christians into pastoral and governing roles. In doing so we exalt their recognition way beyond the development of their character.

Because their gift is dynamic we assume that their ability to govern and lead will be successful. We forget that it takes maturity to be a leader. We forget that it takes wisdom to govern. And wisdom takes time. It takes time to develop, time to be tested, time to be seen and evaluated under fire.

We have to see their servanthood emerge. That also takes testing.

That also takes time.

It's an established fact that sooner or later, we reap what we sow.

* And the Lord knows that if we have not sown faithfulness in the seemingly smaller things, then if He were to give the responsibility of greater things, somewhere down the line there is going to come a reaping and a lot of destruction could be the result.

Faithfulness is not optional, it is vital!

Those in senior leadership roles must allow for the time necessary to see the evidence of these essential Christlike qualities. Take time. The extra commitment is worth it.

REFLECTION

1. Paul said about Timothy, "For I have no one likeminded who will sincerely care for your state". Do you see a lack of servanthood in the Church today? Consider what it would take for this culture to change.

2. Do you feel that people believe that an attitude of servanthood will limit their chances of promotion? If so, why?

3. Paul knew that a person's attitude toward the greater responsibility would be exactly that which they had demonstrated toward the lesser responsibility. How have you served in the 'small' things?

4. How do those you want to promote serve in the 'small' things?

5. In recent years we have seen a trend in placing relatively new young Christians into roles of leadership and recognition. What are the safeguards and principles we should be considering before doing so?

PRAYER

Father, Jesus showed us the greatest example of servanthood when it was said about Him "who being in the form of God, did not consider it robbery to be equal with God, but made Himself of no reputation, taking the form of a servant". Lord at times this is difficult to do. Sometimes it is difficult to "decrease so that You might increase" but I know this is what I am called to do. In fact it's not just a calling but it is my privilege to serve You and to serve others. Please help me to rediscover the absolute joy of serving. Lord help me to ensure this always stays the foundation and motivation of all that I do.

Chapter Six

ACCOUNTABILITY

All true leaders have, as one of their primary aims, the ongoing well being of those that they are to lead. As they see the needs represented, they take steps to ensure that those needs are adequately taken care of.

Jesus saw the needs of mankind and so provided the atonement with His own life. He saw the needs of His disciples on a Sabbath day and released them to provide food and eat. He went on to see the need of His newly-born Church and so provided the person of the Holy Spirit to minister to that need.

The example of Jesus as a leader is one of selflessly providing for the needs of those He came in contact with, and most of all, those for whom He was more directly responsible.

According to Ephesians 5:27 Jesus loved the Church with the knowledge that He would have to present her one day in her perfected state. He lived in the awareness of that responsibility and His life on earth was committed to carrying out that commission.

This is, of course also applicable to those of us who are His delegated authorities.

Hebrews 13:17 confirms this as it talks of those who are in overseeing positions. It states that *"they watch for your souls, as those who must give an account"*. In other words, those who will be held responsible for those placed in their charge.

It has long been said that authority and accountability must go hand in hand.

A person who desires an increase in authority, who has no heart to take responsibility for the outcome of that authority being expressed, is a potential dictator.

And so, within the context of the local church, the principle of accountability is well established. The senior Overseer is accountable to Christ for the members of His church that He places into that Overseers care. That senior Overseer walks with a sense of acute responsibility for those lives. They, in turn, are accountable to that Overseer and must respect that relationship with their transparency and responsiveness.

It is essential here that I comment on a growing voice that is declaring that such an accountability relationship is not necessary and that authority in the local Church is a man-made institution designed by those who wish to dominate others. The fact that it is vulnerable to such abuse does not deny the clear declaration of the New Testament that we are to submit to those genuine leaders He has placed as Overseers in His Church.

The same voices question the validity of attending all Church gatherings and reject all expressions of Church Government. Once again the Word urges us to not neglect our gathering together and makes clear that the early Church met on the first day of the week and that Elders were a recognized pastoral support group to the ministries of the Apostle, Prophet, Evangelist, Pastor and Teacher. It is clear that the Church of Paul's day had structure, order and accountability, but that it was the extension of loving and caring relationships, not the enforcement of law.

Now for a moment let us examine the thought of unity in a local body of believers.

Ephesians 1:22, 23

> *"And God placed all things under his feet and appointed Him to be head over everything for the church, which is His body, the fullness of Him who fills everything in every way."*

"Unity amongst believers in any given local area is so critically essential"

God is corporate. The wonder of the incarnation is that a Godhead of three Persons was made fully manifest via one human expression, Jesus. So the corporate was made known in the singular. Now God reverses the miracle as the singular, Jesus, is made fully manifest in His corporate Body, the church. By "the Church" we refer to every born again believer who is being genuinely regenerated by the internal dwelling of the Holy Spirit.

This then explains why unity amongst believers in any given local area is so critically essential to God and so feared and attacked by Satan. Should the world ever see Christ accurately expressed through the love, selflessness and devotion of His corporate Body, they will respond even as they did when Jesus was that expression *"the common people heard Him gladly"* (Mark 12:36).

Jesus, as expressed through the Church, is the most beautiful, appealing, attractive, irresistible force this world has ever seen. There is no philosophy or religion, no charisma or personality, no demonstration or natural force that can compare with the fully revealed and risen Christ. As we see this with renewed clarity, we will see how great a priority it is for Believers of all persuasion to "dwell together in unity". This does not only mean a fellowship at my local church on a Sunday morning. It means that there is radical and abundant evidence that all Christians within any given local area are respecting, honouring and loving one another in ways so tangible that their entire community can see it, envy it, and be irresistibly drawn to it. Having said that, how is this practically worked out?

Firstly, within the immediate community of those we know and have consistent fellowship with – our family and our friends. Secondly, whatever expression to which you belong that complies with Paul's command, *"Not forsaking the assembling of yourselves together"* (Hebrews 10:25). *"When you are gathered and each one has a Psalm, a hymn, an exhortation"* (1 Corinthians 14:26). *"Overseers should be able to teach"* (1 Timothy 3:2). *"Obey those who rule over you* (Oversight), *and be submissive, for they watch out for your souls, as those who must give account"* (Hebrews 13:17a).

Today we commonly call this expression "The Local Church" and by that mean an identifiable community that, in their gathering together, passionately seek to honour and represent Jesus by fulfilling these clear biblical commands.

It is sad that some of the abuses of power seen in "the Church" over church history and even today have caused such deep rooted disillusionment that some well meaning authors of late have indicated that all such corporate expressions are "the institutionalised Church". They have been staring so long at the misrepresentation of God's intention that they conclude the intention itself cannot be what God had in mind. This has led them to withdrawing from such activity and settling for spontaneous and individual fellowship "as the Holy Spirit leads".

They are right when they declare that mandated, controlled religion is the enemy of one's individual walk with God. They are right when they say that you don't need structures to have personal intimacy with God. They are right when they say that a dependence upon an outward display, behavioural expectations and "church attendance" has robbed believers of their individual and personal intimacy with God and the need to be personally responsible for that intimacy.

However, they are wrong to conclude that because all of this is so, that attendance at a "local Church" with God-given and appointed elders, deacons and pastors etc, is wrong or not to be pursued.

Are they imperfect? Yes. Does it mean that you have to very prayerfully and carefully choose which one you choose to become a functioning part of? Yes. Does it mean that when you do become committed to that community, you will have to be careful in the balancing of your priorities so as to ensure that your spiritual life (all of life actually!) is not a reflection of your Church life but your personal, intimate friendship with Father, Jesus and Holy Spirit? Yes.

But that is the wonder of what God is doing. He is gathering imperfect individuals together as imperfect identifiable communities with imperfect leadership and imperfect programs and by a work of His Holy Spirit, through each of these imperfect individuals, bring that community to a corporate expression of Jesus in the wider community (society) in which they are placed. Such transformation is not achieved by the withdrawal of the passionate, the pure, and the intimacy advocates. It is achieved by them being the salt of that Body and seeing it, in turn, become the salt of the world around them.

Travelling Ministry

But what of those who no longer pastor a flock? Perhaps they have been released in an apostolic role to minister to the Body of Christ at large. Maybe they are now itinerant as a Prophet, Evangelist or Teacher.

It is indeed true that the greater the public acceptance of one's ministry, the greater the vulnerability. This therefore demands that those in prominence in the Kingdom need to establish the principles of accountability.

In Acts 13:1-4 we have Barnabas and Paul sent out by those in leadership at Antioch. In Acts 14 they return to give an account (verses 26 & 27).

> *"They sailed to Antioch, where they had been commended to the grace of God for the work ... reported all that God had done with them."*

It becomes apparent that Barnabas and Paul were not in any way divorced from the principle of accountability. They were ones who knew they were accountable to the elders at Antioch. So should it be for the "travelling ministry" today.

This is not only for the protection of the ministry involved, but also for the churches and groups to whom they will minister. The fact that they are in submission and accountable leads to others having confidence in the potential fruit of their ministry. Host churches have the right to ask who their accountability group are.

A good example being Apollos in Acts 18:27 where *"the brethren wrote, exhorting the disciples to receive him ."*

Paul, many times gives such recommendations of fellow believers and he removes such when they fall from the standards of a Godly life and testimony. Some examples of this are when he rejects the endorsement of Phygellus and Hermogenes and also Hymenaeus and Philetus in 2 Timothy 2:16-18 *"who have strayed from the truth".*

It is obvious that this principle of accountability and its related principle of endorsement are vitally needed today. It would greatly assist in the remedying of the present vulnerability in the Church to "lone-star" ministries if it were more universally applied.

Don Basham puts it this way:

> *"Examining the scriptures, I saw how most false ministries today could be properly dealt with if the Body of Christ could uniformly apply the principle of endorsement."*

He goes on to correctly observe however, that:

> *"Such an idealistic solution to the problem of false ministries is, at the present time, little more than a devout wish. Nevertheless, the principle is scripturally sound, and its application must begin with those who recognise its validity."*

For my own life I have chosen a number of accountability levels: my wife, Margaret comes first, then my son, Steve, and the senior leadership at David McCracken Ministries. Then there is my Board who are all strong, confronting leaders in their own right. I also invite individual Apostolic leaders that both Margaret and my team know are locked into place with me relationally.

"God is seeking to build teams" Margaret and I are also members of CityLife Church and Mark Conner is our Senior Minister with an unqualified right to speak into our lives at any time. There is a sense of security that this brings to those in the Body of Christ considering either receiving our ministry or investing into it.

It is my most fervent conviction that God is seeking to build teams and bring itinerants out of isolation and into an accountability relationship with an apostolic leader who can play a "parental" figure in their lives. If they are themselves already "fathers" or "mothers", then peer group accountability is critical and they should be proactively seeking to pursue it.

Why have I said that accountability is a key in the area of motivational purity in leadership?

* When one knows that the fruit of each decision they make will be subject to the scrutiny of those with the responsibility to be their watchmen, they are less likely to make such decisions in an arrogant or presumptuous manner.

* When they also have a conviction concerning their own appearance before the Judgement Seat of Christ, they are even less likely to so do.

* I believe that most leaders today need a fresh revelation of the awesomeness of God and their own accountability to that same God for the lives of those given into their charge.

Having said all of that, when one comes into true intimacy with Father and shares His devotion towards God's people, accountability is worn no longer as a restrictive harness but as an instinctive and spontaneous expression of a heart yearning to please and gaining great delight in doing so.

REFLECTION

1. With authority comes responsibility. List some areas in which the responsibility of leadership demands involvement in people's lives. What changes in priorities become necessary to actively pursue such an involvement?

2. Talking about leadership, the Bible says *"they watch for your souls, as those who must give an account"* (Hebrews 13:17). In what way do you find that this statement affects the way that you lead?

3. If you are a travelling minister, who do you directly relate to as your apostolic connection and to whom do you submit personally?

PRAYER

Father as we start to explore this principle of accountability I pray that you will always help me act with integrity and total transparency. For those who look to me for accountability, help me to support them well. Help me to submit to those to whom I am accountable to. May my accountability to others be more than a token gesture. I know that I must give an account for the way I treat Your Church; therefore I ask that you help me to always be honourable in my dealings with others.

_____ *Chapter Seven* _____

FOLLOW
ME

With eyes firmly fixed on the back of the one in front of them, they walked through the unknown with blind trust in the one that was leading them. As night fell and the sky seemed to close around them, they realised something was terribly wrong.

They had not only lost their way but now the team leader was feeling desperately ill and unable to continue thinking and leading clearly.

This would not be a problem they thought: "After all, we have among us some extremely gifted and intelligent people!" But as they sat to discuss the situation, it soon became apparent that such had been their dependence and trust upon the team leader, that not one of them had looked at the map nor taken heed to the original instruction given to them at the Rangers Office before proceeding. Each one had assumed that someone else would have checked it all out, and besides, no one anticipated the leader getting sick.

The darkness now seemed to force itself upon them and they realised the futility of the regrets they all were expressing. It was supposed to have been so straight forward: the leader would do all the homework, the leader would study the trail, the leader would tell them what to do, the leader would ensure they got there, the leader was responsible. He had said "follow me" and that, they reasoned, was all they were responsible to do. And now they were lost.

So many today share their fate. People who have gone through life without the internal development of their own initiative potential. Why?

For some it is because that is the way of humanity; the gravitational pull to reliance upon others fuelled by slothfulness and a lack of personal vision.

"Why am I doing what I'm doing, and who am I doing it for?"

But for others, they are the product of being raised in an environment in which the inappropriate motivation of the leader has led to that leader adopting a leadership style that discourages the development of the individual.

Not all such motivation is malicious. Some of it is, in fact, noble and selfless, but terminally misguided.* Any motivation that does not cultivate the greater potential of the individual and inspire that individual's confidence and initiatives, is inappropriate for a leader.

I believe every existing and emerging leader should ask critical questions concerning their motivation in leadership.

 "Why am I doing what I'm doing, and who am I doing it for?"

But why such an emphasis on our motives?

1. It's all-important to God and therefore all-important to the eternal value of what we do.
2. Motivation in leadership will always end up dictating one's philosophy in leadership, which in turn, will determine one's life-expression in leadership or "leadership style". This will then determine the impact of that leadership on the Body of Christ.

There are those who appear to believe that there should not be any type of leadership in the Body of Christ at all because "all people are equal before God". In the words of Judges 21:25, they think it quite fine if everyone does that which is right in their own eyes. This, of course, is firmly refuted by scripture. But what of those who do believe in leadership? Are they all expressing a philosophy that is firmly scripture based?

There are two foundational thoughts upon which we establish our many and varied philosophies of leadership.

Two biblical statements:

1. "Follow me" (Sheep-shepherd concept). Matthew 4:19
2. "Go ye" (Command and direction). Matthew 28:19

Both of these are vital and both of these are correct.

The vulnerability lies when either one of these two is taken in isolation from the other or is not coming from the motivation of a servant heart.

Let us now examine the abuse of the first of these.

Follow Me

Peter Wiwcharruck speaks to this philosophy of leadership in the following way:

> *"From this very simple phrase we can develop a picture*

of Jesus walking up and down the land calling out to the twelve and others, "Follow me". From this we can easily conceive the sheep-shepherd philosophy, and from that produce a 'paternal' or 'pastoral' form of leadership where the shepherd leads and the sheep follow blindly behind.

Now ... if the congregation has been adequately conditioned by tradition and/or leadership action to accept the principle that all authority and responsibility is in the Pastor alone, or an exclusive group at the top, then we see a certain percentage picture emerge ... 80% of the congregation will eventually settle down into a state of spiritual lukewarmness and disinterested inaction; 10% will respond to the follow me in a more positive way; and the other 10% will completely ignore the call, and will wander in their own ways ... often getting lost and into trouble."

The problem with such imbalance is that it will always end up with disillusioned people who are vulnerable to the introduction of resentment and bitterness.

Why? Because they have become casualties of a man-made philosophy of leadership which denies them one of their basic God created desires.

People were created to be "doers".

Created in the likeness of their God, men and women were designed to be a creative, diligent and productive part of whatever community they found themselves in. Every instinct within their newly acquired Christ-nature will arise to confirm this.

When they arrive in the ultimate community, the community of the Church, such instincts will yearn for their rightful expression. And when denied, they simply ferment within and leave that individual vulnerable to picking up further "evidence" that the present leadership are "out of tune" or not "anointed for the job".

It does not take long for bewildered saints to become critical saints.

This abuse of the "Follow Me" principle expresses itself in two different leadership styles which originate out of two different motivational bases (both wrong).

The *servile* which originates in insecurity.

The *aggressive* which originates in greed or ambition.

Let us examine these motivational bases.

So MANY SHOES...So LITTLE TIME.

The Servile

A problem with this concept of leadership is that it makes the leader totally responsible for the welfare and activities of the sheep. Now this may sound very noble, however we must once more investigate the motivation behind such a philosophy.

Basic insecurity and desire to be loved and accepted cause such an individual to work overtime so as to ensure that they are constantly seen by their flock as sacrificial and pastorally caring. They have fallen into the trap of believing that the more you do for people, the more they will love you. Such a one becomes the slave of those they seek to be in favour with. Their priorities are designed to be forever "gaining points" with their people. Once again, the motivation is found wanting.

The goal is self. The need for being considered a hardworking, selfless Pastor is uppermost in their mind rather than the ultimate well-being of their people. *Opinion of others, fear of man, a trap that's to the detriment of those leading/serving*

The result is a disaster. The people are robbed of their own expression and the leader works themself into an early grave or forced retirement.

Obviously, this is not God's intention!

Good leadership is not what you can do *for* the people but what can be achieved *with* the people. This, of course, involves that persons spiritual health and whatever counsel is necessary to achieve that, but with a clear objective of that individual functioning fruitfully in their own ministry expression.

What we do find is that when one's motivation is the cultivation and release of the people to "do the work of the ministry", then one works just as tirelessly (possibly more so at times) but, without a driving compulsion for which the grace of God is not extended! When we work hard with pure motivation and as a result of the Lord's own direct command, then His grace is released in us to be our sufficiency for the task. *Work hard - pure motivation - God's command → God's grace*

Often stemming from a childhood of acceptance and value by virtue of works alone, this insecurity manifests itself in many and varied ways. A good example is of the Pastor who, though insisting everyone else takes adequate holidays, restricts himself to a few days a year. For years we have looked upon this as "selfless serving" rather than what it really is. Our soul and body both demand rest. Those who have done exhaustive studies seem to agree that a minimum one day a week totally separated and apart from the ministry is vital. They also recommend a minimum of four weeks holiday a year. Senior Leaders with heavy and unrelenting responsibilities will probably need more. The majority of Pastors have served for years and years without such a "luxury".

*Take care of yourself, or you won't have much left to give to others.
Also take care of yourself for yourself!

Chapter 7 • Follow Me

When I wrote the original text of this book, some twenty years ago, I was sitting in a Christian Medical Clinic receiving twice weekly treatments for a heart condition. A condition that could have, in part at least, been avoided by the above. My friends, prevention is better than cure.

*If we are secure in our calling, secure in our motivation, secure in our intimacy with Jesus, secure in the knowledge that we work for Him diligently and with dedication of heart; then we will take holidays. We will delegate, we will release others to do the work. We will take time to pray, time to rest and time with the family. The other five or six days in the week we will work zealously for the Kingdom (but without frenzy). The other forty-eight weeks of the year (with the careful provision of sufficient short replenishing breaks) we will joyously run our race with dignity and honour and live to do it again next year!

*If our motivation is to see the needs of the people met and their destiny in God fulfilled, then we can best serve them by being fully alive.

We need to be alive and alert in our daily vigilance, alive and vital in our communication, alive and zealous in our example. People want the inspiration of leadership that is fresh and alive!

*To plan your year to include times of refreshing is not selfish, it is vital to serve the King and His people. Vital for an ongoing, Christ-exalting witness!

Even should one seem to remain healthy while ignoring these principles, there is another issue to consider: *tired Christians are vulnerable Christians. They are vulnerable to the ever-increasing attacks of our adversary in moral and spiritual areas.

*Leaders are not exempt from principles common to us all. In fact, they are much more of a target and are the more vulnerable. When one's emotional, mental and physical resources are depleted there comes the accompanying weariness of spirit. That weariness can result in a lack of alertness and that can be fatal when Satan comes in like a flood!

In addition to times of joy and replenishment, we must be scheduling

Make. The. Time.

*times of personal intimacy with Father and set apart times to see clearly and hear Him speak those words of fresh commission and vision for the days ahead.

In summing up the insecurity element in "follow me" leadership, one would have to conclude that many Pastors today are so busy doing things for the people that they are neglecting their primary responsibility to make something with the people.

*The right motivation will help us refocus on the needs of others and, in so doing, aid us to line up our leadership philosophy with that of Jesus - one of people development.

When we read again Matthew 4:19, we see that the objective of His *"follow me"* was that He might *"make them fishers of men"*.

Here is the key. The motivation of Jesus was not that He might gather a band of people around Him that would be totally dependent on Him to do everything for them and so satisfy His own need to be wanted.

His motivation wasn't Himself, to satisfy & feed His own insecurity, but to equip & prepare His disciples for their callings, destinies

No! His motivation was that He wanted to make something of them! He wanted them to be productive and consequently fulfilled. His job was to equip them. Their ministry and the responsibilities that He

96

knew they had coming up, was the reason that He poured His life into them.

When Jesus called "follow me", it was a call to discipleship and equipping which would involve their acceptance of His leadership and the consequent transformation of their lives from those who existed to be fed, to those who would be empowered to feed others. In following Jesus they were to follow His example and be accountable to Him for the task He was to give them.

Wiwcharuck puts it this way:

> *"The main function of leadership is to make something OF the people, and then let them do what needs to be done. A good leader never does FOR the people what they can do for themselves."*

In Matthew 14:15-21, we have the story of Jesus feeding the five thousand. The point often overlooked, is that Jesus only did what was not possible for the disciples to do.

> *"But Jesus said to them, "They do not need to go away. You give them something to eat". And they said to Him, "We have here only five loaves and two fishes". He said, "Bring them here to Me"... He blessed and broke and gave the loaves to the disciples; and the disciples gave to the multitudes."*

That which was within their own potential to achieve (with supernatural empowerment), He gave them the responsibility to carry out.

It demanded a degree of trust many of them had not used in that way before and it was extremely challenging, but Jesus knew that they had to be stretched a little or they would never have had that experience built into their foundation for a future life of faith.

Even though He was the ultimate expression of humility in a servant, there was nothing passive or servile about the leadership of Jesus. Servility is not servanthood. Servanthood demands strong, decisive leadership that is secure enough to be effective in the constructive moulding of another life in order for that life to fulfil the destiny of God.

When Jesus declared "follow me" He was doing so from the base of selfless love. So secure was he in the knowledge of His uncomplicated motivation for them, He never hesitated to be confronting when it was necessary. His "follow me" style of leadership was designed to cultivate and release an individual into their ultimate potential.

The Aggressive

As previously stated this corruption of the "Follow Me" principle is born out of greed and ambition.

This is where the leader is anything but unaware of the people's potential but sees their potential in the light of how it can best serve their own aspirations! It is to this style of leadership that the "Sauls" of this life gravitate.

They are those who being "head and shoulders above the people" believe that the people exist merely as the means by which they can accomplish their goals, visions and their dreams.

Other than that, the people are of no real personal value as individuals.

Such men tend to see "vision" in the terms of property rather than people, money rather than missions, and man's acclaim rather than man's need.

The consistent emphasis of the pulpit is the need for the people to serve the leadership and their vision. Any questioning of this vision is of course, disloyalty. This leader has no qualms about making it rich at the expense of the people (the opposite of our first example) and sponges up their generosity and giving while never being involved in selfless giving themselves.

It is the people who must sacrifice.

Their glorious calling is the paramount consideration. Friendship with the people is not considered a priority or even desirable. After all, there should be an "appropriate distance" between the clergy and the laity. It "helps them maintain respect for leadership".

What absolute nonsense! How totally contrary to the example of Jesus, who was intimate with His leadership team and allowed children to sit on His knee.

This aggressive nature, once again, reflects in a persons leadership philosophy and style.

You will find that such a one is extremely meeting-orientated. Unfortunately, it is hard to deny the fact that this philosophy has subtly infiltrated even some of our more genuinely motivated Pastors today.

The pressure to gather people is often not a "burden for the lost" but rather the need to have the numbers growing and the church pews filled. It is not a "crying for

> *"They simply do not care, as long as they are entertained"*

the dying" but a chart on the office wall! The gathering of the people is essential if we are to have a "great meeting". The more people you do gather, the more "successful" the meeting is seen to be. The objective is the success of the meeting rather than the ultimate well-being of those attending.

Peter Wiwcharuck makes this comment:

> *"Because the church is basically meeting orientated, the condition is essential to holding meetings where a large proportion of the congregation is willing to sit idly by and watch a performance by a small minority of its membership. If it were not for that 80%, we could not hold meetings regularly. The beauty of this kind of conditioning is that it doesn't matter how lukewarm or dead 80-90% of the congregation is, we can still have*

Not about appearances, but what's really going on underneath - why do what you do & for who?

> *'successful' meetings as long as they come to church! As a matter of fact, the more lukewarm they are, the easier it is on everybody because they are less likely to get disturbed mentally and emotionally by either a poor or a very good sermon."*

What he is saying is that they simply do not care, as long as they are entertained!

When one examines the "Follow Me" principle outworked in the life of Jesus, we have to acknowledge that it involved large and successful meetings. But the magnitude of the crowd was never the objective, life transformation was. Jesus was all about establishing a new kingdom culture in the hearts of men and women and a demonstration of the power of that kingdom. The gathering of them in one place was for singular purpose.

I fully acknowledge the wonderful work being done by many today who have ended up with "mega churches" and reject utterly any suggestion that they are all in some way compromising discipleship in order to get the numbers. Once again, the indication is not the size of the crowd but the degree of Christ-like character and hunger for God that is being achieved by them being there.

What I am saying, however, is that healthy reappraisal by such leaders to ensure that those objectives are not lost in the process of growth is absolutely vital.

Having stated the abuses of the principle, there are several reasons why "follow me" is an important part of good leadership.

I will mention three of these:

1. It is necessary to initially gain our attention and so draw us out of the masses. The leader honestly desiring to make something of the people must first have gained their attention in order to then begin that work of developing their lives. The "follow me" call will gain that attention.

2. The call to identify with a person, or cause, is very important to us being inspired to pay the price and make our break with the security of life as we have previously known it. E.g. the disciples left their boats and their fishing careers in order to obey that call.

3. Our third one comes from Peter Wiwcharuck:

   "By coming out from the crowd and associating ourselves with the specific cause we make ourselves available for teaching and involvement."

   In other words, we become candidates for change.

And so, for these reasons alone, the "Follow Me" principle is a vital aspect of leadership when held in proper balance, and when coming from a heart motivation that is pure and selfless. I again must emphasise that motivation (why you do what you do and who you do it for) is the crucial question that must be answered honestly.

REFLECTION

1. When we work hard with pure motivation and as a result of the Lord's own direct command, then His grace is released in us to be our sufficiency for the task. Do you feel God's grace upon you as you are leading His people? Have you analysed those times when that grace seems to lift? Be careful to avoid any imposing of self-guilt at such times but allow the Holy Spirit to talk with you concerning that.

2. Are you a leader who, though insisting everyone else takes adequate holidays, restricts yourself to a few days a year? How can you change that?

3. Many wear the word 'busyness' as a badge of honour. As one person said, "we are called to be fruitful, not busy". This is the truth and the more 'rested' we are the more fruitful we will be. How are you planning such times of personal replenishment?

4. Identify ways in which you can increase in your capacity to develop the potential of others and see them released more effectively. How are you going to do this?

5. Are there any insecurity issues that leave you vulnerable to one of the abuses mentioned? Who is it that you can now talk that through with?

PRAYER

Father, the motivation of my heart is something that only you and I can truly know. Please search my heart on this area of the 'follow me' principle. Do I have a correct perspective? Am I too servile or too aggressive? If I am please make it clear to me and I know with Your help I can change. I love Your Church and I love Your people. Amen.

_ *Chapter Eight* _

GO
YE

Ted sat deep in thought as the jeep bumped its way toward the frontline and the sound of gunfire became ever closer. "Would these troops accept him as their new commanding officer, they had so loved the previous one and were obviously angry at his removal?"

Ted was concerned.

The more he thought of it, the grimmer the task became and his fears of rejection began to cloud his normally sound judgement. As he played out imaginary scenarios in his mind, his anxiety increased with every compounding thought. By the time he had arrived he was anticipating nothing but problems with those he was supposed to lead.

He was greeted by one of his new team who began to share how he saw the problem and the necessary strategy to initiate. "What is this? I'm here three minutes and he is trying to take my command already!" With a reaction born of his own irrational conclusions, Ted ignored the suggestions and instantly began to rebuke the junior officer and bark out his own orders. The fact that he was unfamiliar with any of the details and that the junior officer was vastly more experienced with both the challenge and the troops, was eclipsed by the perceived need to establish himself quickly and decisively.

As one disaster gave way to another and ground, once won by courage and sacrifice, now was lost, the resentment of the troops continued to grow. From time to time they would try to voice their opinions only to be ignored.

Finally, someone snapped and went straight to the commanding officer. As the investigation commenced Ted sat in grim silence and took the events now unfolding as sure proof that his original fears had been well founded. "I knew they would reject my leadership. Their disloyalty is no surprise to me!"

"Go ye" These are command words and are essential to good leadership.

We all know that many people have an inbuilt reaction against being told where they are to go and what they are to do. That lack of inviting discipleship into one's life has caused so much unnecessary hurt and painful memories. We are designed to live in the security of being under God's command, and He most often expresses that through delegated authority figures in our lives. With children it is their parents, with school children it is (*supposed to be*) their teachers. Isn't it amazing that when we grow up and the responsibility for our decisions are far greater, we assume the arrogance of believing that we need the counsel and wisdom of no one other than ourselves. But that kind of thinking originates with vanity and ends in disobedience and destruction.

The problem is that so many have come from a background of abuse by the very ones they previously trusted for such security. Their experience of a father figure or church leader has often been marred by an example of selfish and even brutal disregard for their wellbeing rather than that of their protector. These ones then come to Christ and carry the trauma of those events into their philosophy of church leadership. They develop a philosophy that will protect them from the potential of such abuse in the future, but in so doing, build walls that successfully keep out the very voices God assigns to help them towards wholeness.

Some people in this category often then shroud their anger at the past and suspicion of the future, with a super spirituality that claims such an intimacy with God personally, that the need of human discipleship or spiritual authority figures are not necessary. Others simply state their case by keeping their distance, ignoring their need for intimacy.

Although they can appear to flourish initially in such an unrestrained atmosphere, sooner or later their rejection of spiritual leadership leads them to a place of isolation from vital checks and balances God has given to keep them walking in truth and reality.

* No matter how long it takes, isolation always breeds error.

* We are created for relationships that include authority, submission and accountability. They are not religious words, they are biblical words.

There are times a leader must say "follow me", but good ongoing leadership has in it more "go ye" than "follow me".

It is all too obvious that insecurities within many a good potential leader has caused their directive voice to lack sufficient conviction to command the respect and response of those they are leading.

Whereas those who are secure, because they have settled within themselves the true nature of their motivation, will not feel the unwarranted need to hold back at such times when a decisive voice needs to be heard.

They will in fact, realise that the entire objective of "follow me" is "go ye".

Peter Wiwcharuck once stated:

> *"It is imperative in this day to get both the leadership and the people to recognise that the Christian Church is not a multitude of small groups of people following all forms of self-made leadership ... heading for a dead end.*
>
> *The Church is the body of Christ! ... chosen and commanded to 'GO'. There is a common commission and a common objective. 'GO YE!' if this then is so (and I believe that it is) it would explain why a church which has an absence of the 'GO YE' element in leadership will normally find that a large percentage of the congregation are idle because they are merely 'following'."*

Their main responsibility is to 'hurry up and wait'."

* It is a soul-destroying experience to be forever stirred to be committed and passionate, but never being given an opportunity to express that passion in a creative and fulfilling manner.

And here lies the balance concerning the "Saul" excesses of "Follow me" (chapter 7).

In no way was I seeking to convey that strong, dynamic leadership is wrong. Strong, dynamic leadership that is God appointed, God anointed and comes from a pure motivation of heart, is God's primary tool in the perfecting and releasing of His Church.

Without strong leadership, there will be no discipleship.

Without strong leadership, there will be no spiritual maturity.

Without strong leadership, there will be no commissioning.

Without strong leadership, there will be no vital adjusting.

Without strong leadership, there will be only gypsies.

And worst of all, without strong leadership, passionate individuals will never be welded into the ranks of His army and therefore released to effective warfare. Instead, their passion will blaze away like a fire unattended and end up corrupting the vessel rather than empowering them for service.

Strong leadership releases.
Strong leadership is not insecure, not self-preserving, not self-promoting.
Strong leadership is about Jesus & people.

God is raising up His great end-time battalions, His troops of power, His ultimate weapon to crush Satan's head. They will <u>not</u> be <u>independent</u> individuals <u>doing their own thing</u>, they will be <u>those who know where God has appointed them for training and to whom He has given them for that training.</u> *Interdependent race - running with, not against each other*

And so, "Go Ye" is absolutely vital.

However, in acknowledging this, we must also point out the vulnerability of this philosophy if not coming from the heart of one who has first known the road of true servanthood.

Though this style of leadership will ultimately get more done for the Kingdom of God, it also carries in it the potential to be abused and to become an affliction rather than a blessing to the people of God.

When the "Go Ye" philosophy comes from a <u>heart not yet broken</u> and <u>soft to the Master's touch, the result can be decisions made presumptuously and without due regard to the sensitivities and wellbeing of the individual who that one is commissioning.</u>

The <u>achieving of the objective becomes more vital than the ultimate fruitfulness of the one being sent.</u> Such leaders are extremely "<u>goal orientated</u>" and have little tolerance of those who do not do well in the task given. The harsh treatment of some of those who have not particularly excelled is, once again, an expression of the "Saul nature".

Let me give an example of what occurred early in my ministry years.

The Outburst of a Tyrant

In the company of well respected men of God, I was allowed to attend a Pastor's Conference in another country. Wow! I had been in the senior leadership role in my own local church for just a few short months and this was a great honour. I could hardly wait.

The day arrived and the opening session was powerful singing, fellowship, praise; it was all quite overwhelming.

Then the host pastor (Chairman of the Conference) stood up for the opening address. We all waited with expectation. He started talking of missions and their vital part in his vision for his church. He went on about how great and marvellous his leadership in this field was.

He then singled out one young missionary who had not done well and had to return home. What a disgrace he was to their glorious vision, a blot on their record, a betrayer of the cause. And on and on!

The young man's wife was present. She fled the auditorium in tears and my respect and admiration for this "great man of God" fled with her. I well remember the anger, the indignation, the hurt and the disillusionment. The man was one of the past giants of the faith. What had gone wrong?

The Saul had taken over. The need to have his reputation and his vision admired had eclipsed his pastoral concern. Pride and arrogance had driven out his sensitivity to the sweet voice of a caring, loving Father's heart.

I don't know what happened to the young missionary and his wife, but I do know the end of that Saul. Some years later that man was disgraced, broken and rejected. Like Saul of old, his end was in infamy rather than honour. What a tragedy. Oh that we could prevent the development of such in the primary stages!

"Such a mentality for kingdom building will not find reward"

Acceptance comes by virtue of one's performance for the cause rather than one's personal value as an individual. Such a mentality for kingdom building will not find reward in the heart of the Great Shepherd Who "gave Himself for the sheep".

Having said that, it must be emphasised again, that the Great Commission that Jesus gave His Church, absolutely depends upon the "Go Ye" element being the more active of the two principles.

※ The challenge is to embrace it with a heart that is also motivated as a shepherd; loving, caring and nourishing those being trained for the task.

Jealousy

Our understanding of what can take the heart of a man of God today and make him a Saul would be incomplete if we did not examine the subject of jealousy.

1 Samuel l8:6-13. As you look at this chapter, you will find that jealousy has within it a progression, a development of its evil. Saul (Verse 8) is seen to be angry and when that anger is not dealt with, it gives way to suspicion. (Verse 9) suspicion, in turn, gave way to fear. (Verse 12) fear, the Bible tells us, has torment (obsession).

The fear produced by jealousy will then seek to drive a man to try and eliminate the object of that fear.

The vulnerability of strong leaders today is that in their ranks, there are emerging younger men and women upon whom the anointing rests heavily. As the reality of God's hand upon them is more and more evident, the response of God's people confirms it.

It is so easy now for that older leader to feel threatened as they see the recognition and popularity of this emerging leader. What they do at such a point is critical.

They can rejoice with the emerging "David" and, in acknowledging the destiny upon them, seek to serve that destiny with a selflessness of heart.

To do this is to make the transition with honour and create for themselves an ongoing supportive role as "parent" and counsellor.

However, should they resist and allow the seeds of jealousy and competition to take root, the outcome will be tragedy. There will be pain and trauma to the one emerging and the spiritual death sentence of a Saul upon that leader.

When such a one still retains the "right" to rule over God's people, the ultimate result is the kind of tyranny that has scattered sheep all over this world. Such a leader must come to a place of realisation and honesty that leads them to repentance.

However, it must be stressed that a legalistic adherence to a self-imposed righteousness or humility will not produce a "David" out of a "Saul".

There has to be that moment of personal revelation, that encounter with one's "burning bush". There has to be that moment when the Lord gains our attention and we are faced with the reality of our true condition and see its desperate need for change.

We can clearly see this in the time of fresh challenge and commission that God brought into the life of Isaiah.

Isaiah 6:1, 5-9

> *"Then I said: 'Woe is me, for I am undone! Because I am a man of unclean lips, And I dwell in the midst of a people of unclean lips, For my eyes have seen the King, The Lord of hosts.' Then one of the seraphim flew to me, having in his hand a live coal which he had taken with the tongs from the altar. And he touched my mouth with it, and said: 'Behold, this has touched your lips; Your iniquity is taken away, And your sin purged'. Also I heard the voice of the Lord, saying: 'Whom shall I send, And who will go for Us?' Then I said, 'Here I am! Send me'. And He said, 'Go and tell this people'."*

First, there had to be that awesome moment of revelation and Isaiah's unqualified response. Only then could the fresh commissioning take place.

Frank Damazio speaks to this thought:

> *"Every leader should be a man that the Lord Jesus can visit by His Spirit in such a way that he will make Jesus the full Lord of his life, humble himself before Christ, worship Him, and allow an understanding of the Lord's holiness to cause every impure fetter to be shaken loose from his life.*
>
> *Such visitations are for the purpose of a leader being a more pure vessel for the Lord's work."*

It's not about you. Jentzen Franklin's pizza box example - you're just the vessel - be empty & clean for the Lord's work.
God's heart is for people, not performance benchmarks, goals, profits, etc.
Jesus came for people.
Interdependent relay, not competition. Equip, train up, disciple, release, encourage - run together, not against.

REFLECTION

1. The leader who abuses the 'Go Ye' principle sees the achieving of the objective as more vital than the ultimate fruitfulness of the one being sent. What steps can you take to ensure that this does not happen in the outworking of your own leadership?

2. Is there an emerging leader that you know God is anointing greatly for the task ahead? Is it possible that God has been speaking to you about an adjustment of roles or the delegating of areas of responsibility?

3. Has God visited you recently and does He have your permission to search your heart and challenge you in the areas of truth, transparency and personal purity? Do you have those with whom you can discuss such issues?

PRAYER

Father, Jesus is the Great Shepherd. His love for people is my example. Sometimes it's easy to lose sight of the individual in pursuit of getting the job done. I commit afresh today to always honour people as You honour them. Also I ask that You make it clear to me how I should treat the emerging leaders that You have entrusted into my care. Lord I ask that you search my heart afresh. It is my pleasure to serve You and to serve Your wonderful Church. Help me to always honour You.

_____ *Chapter Nine* _____

The CROSS
FACTOR

Many years ago we had a most traumatic season (to which I have already made reference) when a building program went wrong and people were hurt and shaken. I remember how well meaning people assured me that I had done nothing wrong; that it was the fault of circumstances and other people. Above all, I should now show a strong decisive front to the people.

But God had made me senior overseer and it was the people that the Lord had granted into my care that were hurting. That made me responsible. I knew that somehow in the midst of it all, God was testing my own integrity - my own response of heart to this work of His cross.

This was for us what many would call "the dark night of the soul".

Why do so many strong leaders experience this kind of a dramatic contradiction?

The "Saul's" of this life are often great visionaries, but lack the two ingredients that Jesus (the greatest of all leaders) showed in abundance … true humility and a selfless love for others.

For this reason, the Lord in His mercy will endeavour to bring seasons of the cross into the lives of such potentially strong leaders.

Seasons which, in themselves, may well seem to be contradictions hard to explain; yet without them that individual would not undergo the necessary brokenness of spirit from which the fragrance of humility can later flow.

Quoting yet again from George Warnock:

> *"For it is in the full recognition of all that we are in the realm of weakness and failure that we may reach out and grasp hold of the Divine promises. It is only when Jacob is smitten in the place of strength, 'in the hollow of his thigh' that he finally submits to defeat, and clings*

to the angel of God. And it is only in his defeat, and in clinging to the angel after his defeat, that his name is changed from one of Weakness (contender) to one of Power (Prince with God)."

What a tragedy that so many potential "Israel's" choose rather to cling to their own fierce independence and self-sufficiency. Such Jacobs avoid the cross at all costs claiming that even its discussion is an indication of negative thought.

Thank God for those who, not only knowing His acts but also His ways, accept this vital time of adjustment and persevere to bring to us the testimony of their overcoming faith.

Joseph experienced rejection by his own brothers, false accusation, treachery and thirteen years of wrongful imprisonment. Yet he was a man who kept his integrity and possessed his high calling. He knew that if he kept the purity of his heart toward God, then God would ensure that everything would work eventually to fulfil the destiny and vision God placed in his heart. Joseph believed in the sovereignty of his God. He believed that his life was firmly in His hand.

In Genesis 45:8, he declares to his brothers:

"So now it was not you who sent me here, but God!"

Oh, that you and I could settle this issue!

Moses was one who was uprooted from all he had known to stand up for a people that (correctly) branded him a murderer. Rejected by Egypt and Israel alike he wanders into a wilderness of sore testing for forty years. Yet he kept fast his integrity and when the hour of his burning bush arrived, a deliverer was born.

Paul endured hatred, shipwrecks, imprisonments and even the betrayal of brothers, yet he counted it all joy. Such was his passion to know his Saviour and his love for the Church. Nothing else mattered.

We see this incredible selfless love for the Church in 2 Corinthians

11:23-29, and how it kept his constant challenges in perspective.

> *"Are they ministers in Christ I am more, in labours more abundant, in stripes above measure, in prisons more frequently, in deaths often. From the Jews five times I received 39 stripes. Three times I was beaten with rods. Once I was stoned, three times I was shipwrecked, I spent a night and a day in the deep, in journeys often, in perils of water, in perils of robbers, in perils of my own countrymen, in perils of the gentiles, in perils in the cities, in perils of the wilderness, in perils on the seas, with false brethren in toils with sleeplessness often, in hunger and with thirst, in fasting often, in cold and in nakedness."*

And yet with all of that happening, he declares his deep concern for God's people. Listen to what he said after all that:

> *"and besides all the other things what actually comes upon me daily is my deep concern for all the churches. Who is weak and I am not fainted to feel weak and do I not burn with indignation."*

In the middle of being beaten, stoned, imprisoned and everything he was going through, what was the thing he was most conscious of at any given time? When he was receiving thirty-nine stripes from a guy with a whip with lead pieces, you would have thought that he would have been most conscious of his back. But, Paul said, above all these things that he was going through, the thing he was more conscious of daily, was his deep concern for all the churches.

> *"Who is made to stumble that I do not burn with indignation."*

That is strong terminology!

In the middle of everything that he was going through, the thing that impassioned him was not his circumstance, was not the trial, and was not the floggings: it was the state of the church that burned like a fire inside of him.

The hardships he endured were not things that corrupted his spirit with resentment and a sense of injustice, but rather events that he responded to with an overwhelming sense of privilege at being called to suffer for the Christ and His Church (those he loved with such passion).

"The burden that is ripping God's heart apart: the cries of a lost humanity"

2 Corinthians 2:4

> *"for out of much affliction and anguish of heart, I wrote to you with many tears not that you should be grieved but that you should know the love with which I so abundantly love you."*

This is not a task to this man; this is an experience of abundant love! Is this how we feel about the church?

I have come to the conclusion, the reason why the church is as it is today and ministries have not been more effective than they have been, is because of selfish humanity; because the world exists as a selfish planet and so much of the Church in the West is not a great deal different. It is basically selfish and it is more concerned about itself and self needs than it is for the burden that is ripping God's heart apart: the cries of a lost humanity.

Winning the lost never has been a problem to a church that is on fire, to a church that is impassioned.

It should not be surprising to us that the Chinese Church today is so incredibly healthy and strong. With constant persecutions endured with a sense of privilege, they have learnt that such times only exist to forge the overcoming life of Christ within them more powerfully.

The "Davids" are those who respond Godward in such times and, in realising that *"the steps of a righteous man are ordered of the Lord"*

121

(Psalm 37:23), receive the enlargement, enlightenment or adjustment to their character that He had intended.

 * Such adjustment goes on to prepare a heart to be more able to handle with meekness the developing nature of His authority and power once it is given.

At the time of the original writing of this in 1989 I was half way through my recovery period from my first battle with Coronary Artery Disease and burnout. This is what I wrote then and even as I write this I realise we are never beyond the need for such seasons.

> *"It has now been four months since I have ministered due to a heart condition. Many have shared their persuasions: some with sensitivity and insight and some with good old 'Pentecostal hoot-nanny hype!' It would be so easy to allow frustration to mar the process of the Lord's intention.*
>
> *Yes, I must claim healing in faith. Yes, I must bind every work of the adversary but also, I must (and do) reaffirm that "the steps of a good man really are ordered by the Lord". This is another season of knowing Him in new depth, learning a new facet of His intention. What a terrible waste not to use such an hour to be drawn to Him; to venture beyond the veil to seek out His beauty and wonder. And, in the midst of such a quest, allow the conviction of His scrutiny to remove still more of that unwanted Saul from my heart. In His time, I will minister again but how I cry that I will not be the same limiting vessel; that the sweet work of His cross will have prepared this heart to be more finely tuned with His own."*

That was 1989 but I would say it the same way today.

The "Sauls" are those who, in not responding Godward, react manward in such times and, in losing sight of the cross, allow negative emotions to arise within their hearts. *If you leave negative emotions unchecked they develop into negative character.

Because of a wrong concept of what constitutes strength, they see any breaking or backing down in the situation, to be a response of weakness. Their need to remain "a strong leader in front of people" is a thinly veiled expression of a deep-rooted problem of pride and insecurity. Put quite simply there is a lack of genuine humility. Reactions of hurt and anger give way to a hardening of their sensitivity toward God and others.

Looking back at my own "dark night of the soul", I remember the day came that the elders and I stood before the people and I asked their forgiveness for the distress caused. I knew then in the midst of brokenness, the warmth and tenderness of His acceptance.

So much more heartache and misunderstanding was yet to come, but from that moment I knew the choice was clear. To pick up the sword and defend "my rights" and hence remove myself from the intimacy of His presence; or to leave vindication in His hand alone and pursue but one goal, the pleasing of His heart.

Thank God for the wonders of His grace. Though our hearts were broken and many tears were shed, they served only to ultimately draw Margaret and I closer together and closer to the Father we loved. We now look upon that season as a reservoir of identification and understanding when ministering to other leaders facing their own contradictions of the pastoral life.

What a loss it would have been to have not experienced it at all. Or worse still, to have allowed our anguish and perplexity to have run unchecked and open the door to anger and bitterness. To do so would have been to re-establish the lordship of our own humanity and so rob ourselves (and many others) of the riches and beauty that we can now draw from that season. I call such times "transitions".

REFLECTION

1. The Lord in His mercy will endeavour to bring seasons of "the cross" into the lives of all believers, particularly those in leadership. Have you seen this happen in your life?

2. During your time of darkness, did you respond Godward or react manward? What was the result?

3. Is the fact that *"the steps of a good man are ordered by the Lord"* (Psalm 37:23) a non-negotiable conviction for you as it was with Joseph, Moses, Paul and David?

4. It was said of Abraham that *"he considered Him faithful who had made the promise"* (Hebrews 11:11). Is your focus and trust on the promises of God or the God who gave the promises?

PRAYER

Father, I know that the life of Jesus was anything but easy. There were many trials that He faced and endured. In my own life there have been those times also and I know that there will be more. Therefore I do not ask that You just get me through these challenges but that You will teach me what You want to teach me and as a result help me to become more like You. Help me to honour You by responding Godward and not reacting manward. Help me to have a complete revelation that You order my steps: the good and the not-so-good. Help me not to react against the instrument but rather keep my eye on the Surgeon directing the instrument. You are a faithful God and I completely trust You.

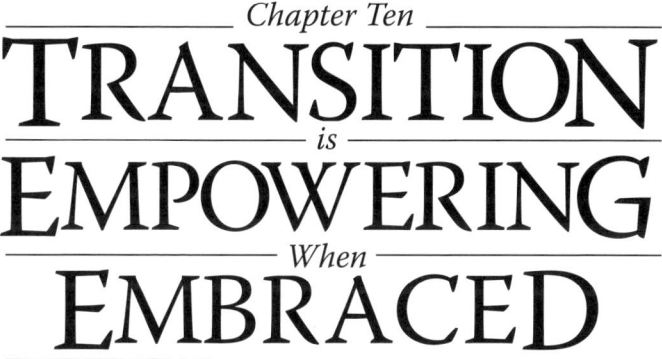

Chapter Ten

TRANSITION
is
EMPOWERING
When
EMBRACED

I live in a quiet road of one acre blocks and well established homes with lots of trees. Whenever out walking I thank my Father for such magnificent evidence of His Designer's touch. Beauty is everywhere and it is awesome to see His creativity as one season gives way to another. With the beauty of autumn, I see the intrusion of red slip amongst the green and deep hues of colour that have me silently in awe at such a visual feast. I love trees and I love autumn. But what can compare with the dawning of spring? Spring is a declaration of life and new potential whose colour may not be as deep but is vivid and wonderfully expressive. Spring is a time of hope, resurrection, fruitfulness and the energy of that which has refused to stay dead. I may love autumn but I come so totally alive with the smell of spring!

But there has to be that which links these two magnificent seasons together. It is the transition called "winter". Without winter, we would stay in the beauty of autumn but never experience the beauty of spring.

Billy Graham once said, *"Mountaintops are for views and inspiration but fruit is grown in the valleys".*

I would like to suggest to you that a valley is a place of transition between two mountaintops. It is that necessary terrain that takes us from the height achievable yesterday to the greater height achievable tomorrow. As we pass through the valley, it is there and there alone that the strength, preparation, enlargement of heart and spirit necessary to scale tomorrow's greater height is gained. It is in the transition of the valley that the fruit is grown and the spirit of conquest is forged that empowers us to scale the greater height.

Transition is empowering when embraced.

The definition of transition is "movement, or change from one position, state, subject, season, concept, etc., to another; change (e.g. the transition from adolescence to adulthood)".

Transition is designed to be the connecting cord between what has been good to what will be far greater, from fruit to extravagant fruit, from days of sufficiency to days of abundance.

Ecclesiastes 3:1-8 tells us our lives are designed to go in seasons. Seasons are all about change, about handling the transition from one state of being to another.

But here is where the challenge lies, because there is something inbuilt within all of us that fears transition because it fears relinquishing, letting go, and the loss of the familiar. The familiar things become our security. Humanity feels more secure in retaining the existing season, the existing DNA, the existing personality or gifting, the existing building or project, rather than reaching out for what is new.

So what is God to do if He is to honour His commitment to our finishing the course with honour and fulfilling the destiny He has for

[handwritten margin notes:] We don't like change, even if it's good-better for us

Something far greater lies on the other side of God's transitions for our lives if we'll just trust Him & embrace what He's doing in these seasons us? He allows some event or season that strips away the confidence and the contentment of that former or existing season. In His devotion to loving us, He pries our fingers open so that the false security of the familiar can float away beyond the potential of our reach. Winter comes, and it can be devastating if it's not understood. Friends, winter is not the cancellation of autumn, it is the preparation for spring!

I find that days of transition are days of questions, of feeling vulnerable and insecure. Days when you desperately need to refocus on God's faithfulness and God's integrity. Your trust in Him has to go to a new level in times of transition.

Transition is a time of change. Transition is when we go from familiar to the unknown, from the secure to the vulnerable. It's the reason why so many avoid it rather than embrace it. Transition is scary!

But transition is inevitable if we are to grow.

Transition touches all of our lives at various moments and can touch every area of who we are and our personal world. It must. If transition isn't allowed to change your heart and your personal world, it has failed in its objective, because it is all about changing you! It is all about the preparation of your heart for the new season of God.

"Transition is empowering when embraced"

And so transition can vary greatly in its duration because transition is all about preparation for the increased authority God intends to give and that is uniquely individual. *Duration of transition is unique to the individual*

Perfect examples of this are two men, equally called of God – Jonah and Moses.

For Jonah the transition/transformation process was three days and three nights. But for Moses it was forty years.

Why? Moses had been raised and trained in the ways of Egypt for forty years! It was the only world he had ever known and God had to undo all of that and then retrain him. The transformation necessary was far more fundamental and deep rooted. It was an entire recreation of who he was as a person and that takes time!

But it was also to do with their commission. For Jonah it was the preparation to preach to a city. For Moses it was the preparation to confront the greatest military force in the known world of its day, deliver millions of people from slavery and then lead them with signs, miracles and wonders for forty years.

Both assignments were of great significance and equally the fruit of obedience. However, the size of the commission determined the nature and duration of the preparation.

✳ Times of transition are God's appointed times for transformation, the preparation of an individual's heart to have the capacity for tomorrow's commission.

Transition is a given; our response to it is up to us

Friends, we do not have the choice of whether or not we will face transition – transition will come! But we do choose our response, which determines the outcome of the transition. The choice of transition is not ours, but the choice of its consequence is.

All our lives we have known times of transition. We all as children faced the transition from Primary (or Junior) School to Secondary (or Senior or High) School.

Times in which, if we had not been willing to leave our friends in Primary School, we would never have discovered our friends in Secondary School.

> *"Transition is all about trust."*

Secondary School became a place of greater empowerment because we embraced the need for that transition. If we had sat in our first year in Secondary School and resented that transition, it would never have empowered us. Yes it was hard at the time but the decision to embrace the transition can and often is hard! It can be hard when you embrace a fundamental change in life.

However transition is always empowering when embraced.

Transition demands courage because it demands letting go. It demands a new level of trust. What gives a Christian that kind of courage, that kind of faith? I believe it is a promise from God.

Psalm 37:23

> *"The steps of a righteous person are ordered by the Lord."*

✳ Courage comes out of a conviction concerning God's faithfulness and His commitment to direct your life.

✳ Transition is all about trust. Trust goes to a whole new level!

Furthermore, transition is designed to be a time of birthing, a conceiving and a bringing forth.

I believe many of you are in a season of birthing. Birthing the new chapter, birthing the future destiny, the future DNA. Let me first give you the context.

In John 16 the disciples were being faced with transition. From three and a half wonderful years with Jesus to the awesome Holy Spirit in the Book of Acts. But in between walking with the Master and being empowered by the Holy Spirit, there was a transition of the Garden and the Cross - the dark night of the soul.

Peter had to go from one who had the boldness to walk on water to becoming an Apostle of faith and wisdom. In between were the Garden and the Cross. Being so confronted with the ugliness of his humanity he wept bitterly, a broken man. But, friends, God wasn't finished with Peter, He was preparing him!

And Jesus, knowing this, addresses it in John 16:21, 22

> *"A woman giving birth to a child has pain because her time has come but when her baby is born she forgets the anguish because of her joy that a child is born into the world. So with you: Now is your time of grief, but I will see you again and you will rejoice, and no one will take*

away your joy."

I want to declare to you that you are pregnant with tomorrow's potential. But for there to be a birthing of it there is always that uncomfortable change in the body, that internal struggle, that travail, that transition that brings the body from the point of conception to birth.

The tragedy is that there are those who are robbed of the promise because of the fear of the struggle that birthing brings, the need for change confronts them. Some people abort the process rather than face the need for change. So they draw back from that transition and shelter themselves in the familiar, the way things used to be. They do not embrace seasons of transition and change and consequently are not empowered by them. God's intention is not realised.

Transition is empowering when it is embraced! But only when it is embraced.

When you reject the need for that transition, you reject the increase that that transition was destined to birth in your life. And when you mishandle that transition, you corrupt that birthing process and its intended result. But God intended that transition to empower you and your relationship with Him.

Transition tests the motives and attitudes of the human heart. It is in times of transition, with all of its shaking and questions, that motives which have laid dormant deep within are brought to the surface for all to see.

Transition is often a time of controversy or contradiction, a time when relationships become vulnerable and commitments fragile. God reveals the true hearts of men and women in times of transition.

The Caterpillar

Imagine a caterpillar. This particular caterpillar was not like any average caterpillar, it was beautiful, colourful, to be admired. But then there came a yearning inside, the birthing of a vision to fly. It thought "wouldn't it be awesome to fly like those birds up there, far above the restrictions imposed upon us down here". So what does it do? Does it sprout wings and take off? No. It goes into a cocoon. It loses its colour, it seems to become dormant, and it goes into a time of inactivity when all its former beauty and grace seem to have been stripped away from it. It appears almost lifeless as it is now anchored to a branch as a chrysalis going nowhere.

What has happened to it? It is in transition.

It may appear tragic but some awesome God-given instinct tells the caterpillar to embrace this transition. It doesn't try to detach itself to continue to crawl as caterpillars do. It submits to that season of transition.

Then, at a God-given moment an urging of life within it begins a time of travail, of birthing and bringing forth. To those looking on, it appears that someone should step in and help but to do so would be to abort the process. That internal struggle, that travail, is in fact the very thing that is creating the beauty that is to come. The final chapter in the transition season is the travail, the struggle to bring forth the new life. The travail is vital! It's producing the new life! Birthing that new beginning depends upon it! Those conditions are necessary and bring about a deeper intensity of prayer – that crying out for God.

But then, suddenly, wonder of wonders, a butterfly emerges and after a short while of drying and recovery from the travail, it spreads its wings and flies in all of its splendour and magnificent colour. The vision birthed in that caterpillar has become a living reality.

The original caterpillar was a thing of beauty and grace. It was created in its own right. But its season of transition eventuated in the birthing of its greater potential and released it to fly! It had to embrace the change. A butterfly doesn't look anything like a caterpillar. But one gave birth to the other!

Nature understands the transition. Every year all of Creation delves into the depths of winter via the intense transition of autumn, only to travail its way into the freshness and new life of spring and ultimately into the joy and fullness of summer.

Our lives will often take a similar course. From a triumph, we find ourselves often moving into a time of discomfort or change. This can take us into a time of struggle and challenge and we long for the previous triumph and the joy we experienced there.

But if we would only embrace that moment and look forward to God's greater purpose of bringing us into a season of even greater fruitfulness, we would see the transition for what it really is and we would begin longing for the new life that is being birthed. We would start dreaming about and working diligently towards the coming joy. We would embrace the transition and open our hearts to the work that our Heavenly Father in His awesome love is wanting to do in us so that we are ready for the spring and the summer.

We must understand that transition and travail are not an indication of God's absence but a confirmation that a new day of promise is on its way. It is the process of that transition that will empower you to fly in your new God given season.

Transition is empowering when embraced, but when you react to the process (the changes being demanded of you, the contradictions that confront you), you are reacting against the Author of that change. Your reaction or your reluctance then disconnects you from receiving the wonderful flow of His grace that He has so abundantly supplied for you in that season. Nothing is as cruel as a graceless transition.

"Nothing is as cruel as a graceless transition"

But when you respond positively and embrace that change in those days of transition, your attitude keeps the valve wide open and His grace so freely given, has its loving, replenishing empowering effect in your life.

Not only is the future outcome of that transition glorious but the work God does in you during the process itself, is beautiful, powerful and eternal. That is when the caterpillar dies and the butterfly is forged.

*There is a depth of experiencing God in pain and travail that transcends anything we know in times of rejoicing. These are the 'wells in the desert', the 'treasures discovered in darkness', these are the moments in which all pretence and all insincerity are stripped away and in a state of spiritual and emotional nakedness, we stand before God unashamed and desperate for His love.

The intimacy possible in such times does not depend upon emotional highs or sensations of wellbeing. It is a deep inner awareness of being loved by our Father, of being held in His embrace of unconditional acceptance and care.

When no argument is convincing, when no evidence is apparent, there comes the assurance of an unreasonable faith 'my Father loves me!'

The beauty and depth of character forged in such times will remain with us forever, and will become a well of life for others to drink from, others who are questioning their time of transition.

All of life is seasons and seasons demand a transition from one thing to another. Perhaps some of you can identify an area in which you are undergoing such a transition right now – vocation, marriage, ministry, finance and relationships, even in who and what God wants you to be. Or perhaps I'm describing something that has already taken place and right now is the climax of that and you are experiencing the travail, the birthing. For all of you, I have a word of encouragement from the Lord and I want to keep it before you.

"You are birthing a new day of promise!"

God has not forgotten you. You are going from "Bearing Fruit" to "Bearing Extravagant Fruit". It is on its way and it is God's intention that it will come right on time.

Jeremiah 33:1-3

> *"Moreover the word of the LORD came to Jeremiah a second time, while he was still shut up in the court of the prison, saying, "Thus says the LORD who made it, the LORD who formed it to establish it (the LORD is His name): 'Call to Me, and I will answer you, and show you great and mighty things, which you do not know.'"*

The reason why God had to bring the word to Jeremiah the second time was because of where he was – shut up in prison. Jeremiah was not preaching to the crowd, declaring the awesome prophetic truths God had granted him, he was locked up in a prison! What a contradiction to all that he had believed for.

But prisons do not need to be places of discouragement and despair. Are they not also part of God's master plan at times?

Let me quote from 'The Leadership Secrets of Billy Graham' (pg 175-176).

> *"Solzhenitsyn, who wrote some of his great novels in brutal work camps, once declared 'Thank God for prison'."*

"Chuck Colson's life was revolutionized by his time in prison and subsequent experience with Christ."

"John Bunyan wrote his classic 'Pilgrim's Progress' in jail."

"Jim Bakker, whom the Graham's befriended during and after his prison experience, became a changed and greatly deepened man during his years in prison."

Prison rescued Jim Bakker. He came forth a transformed man. He was a man who embraced his transition.

Some of you may feel your transition has gone on for a little too long and the devil has suggested it is too late for you.

John chapter 11 is the story of the death of Lazarus.

It appeared that this was one transition that had gone on too long. The subject had died! Martha was understandably upset "Lord, if You had been here, my brother would not have died. If you had only intervened earlier, we would not have gone through this death experience!"

But the reply of Jesus thunders down through the centuries and penetrates the darkest gloom today – it is NEVER too late! You are about to witness a resurrection! The reason I allowed it is because Lazarus had not only a message to deliver but a message to become. When he comes out of that tomb, he will be the message! A message no one will be able to neither refute nor deny!

Whatever season you are in God always has a purpose. We must learn to trust Him and embrace those times of transition, because transition is empowering when embraced.

REFLECTION

1. Have you ever had a dream that now seems dead? Examine the birth of that dream. If it was confirmed at that time as a genuine word from the Lord to your heart, then let hope come alive again! Sit back and allow the Lord to bring it back to you.

2. In the light of what you have read in this chapter, can you think of past transitions that you may have misjudged? Is it possible that what the Lord allowed them for is still able to be realised as you now ask Him to?

3. If you are in the valley between two mountains, ask God to show you clearly the preparation and enlargement that He has placed there for you to embrace.

PRAYER

Father I am uncomfortable with this time of transition I am in, and often my instinct is to run away from it and fight to regain my past triumphs and to enjoy them a little longer. But I know you have a higher purpose to take me into, a season of greater fruitfulness and a deeper relationship with you. I choose right now to embrace that purpose. May your Holy Spirit empower me as I daily live out that choice.

Chapter Eleven

REJECT
Not The
FATHERS

In the relationship between Elijah and Elisha, we see how God's intention for transition is to be both honouring to the Elijah figure and empowering to the emerging Elisha figure.

In 2 Kings Chapter 2 we find some absolutely vital principles that will aid us all in making our own transition with honour. Let me clearly state here that by the term "fathers" I include the thought of "mothers" much like God includes women in His addresses to "man" in the sense of mankind. Spiritual authority is not an exclusively male thing and some of the finest examples of it are the "mothers" among us. So "father" is the nature of the relationship, not an exclusion to women expressing it.

We are approaching the time here when the Elijah era was about to give way to the Elisha era and this meant a fresh move of God.

2 Kings 2:1

> *"And it came to pass when the Lord was about to take*
> *up Elijah into heaven by a whirlwind that Elijah went*
> *with Elisha from Gilgal."*

I believe this is where we are right now in the Body of Christ. There is the desperate need for God to birth something fresh and new in the Body of Christ if we are going to see the fullness of the stature of Jesus Christ; if we are going to see the end time church of Kingdom dominion and authority rise up in the earth. I refer to the power and dominion of a spiritual kingdom, a spiritual reality. If we are believing for that to take place, and I trust that we are, then what we have had up to this point is simply insufficient. Though we are grateful for it, though we appreciate it, though we rejoice in all that God has done and is doing, we are hungry for more.

There must come a fresh move, a fresh breath of revelation into the Body of Christ. Prophetically, I believe we are speaking about the Triumphant Church coming to the *"fullness of the stature of Jesus Christ"* (Ephesians 4:13).

Any fresh visitation of God that does come to the Church will not only affect the lives of individuals (although that is the paramount thing) but as God touches an individual life, it will go on to touch every realm of the Church as well. We must be prepared for that. The attitudes of yesterday have got to go as God now anoints men and women who have intimacy with His heart, those who walk not with an anointing granted because of their office, but an anointing born out of their intimate relationship with the Father.

Change is inevitable and it will touch leadership style; it will touch convictions of the Church; it will touch structure. We long for it and we reach out to receive it.

However let me say this, although such a time is a time of great expectation and joyful anticipation, it is also a time of apprehension and it is a time of vulnerability.

George Warnock says:

> *"In the process of Christian development we are constantly entering transition periods wherein God would take us out of the old and bring us into the new. And it is in this interim period, this transition, this overlapping of the Divine dealings with us, that causes us so much perplexity. We are loath to relinquish the old, till we have the new in our grasp. We would fain enter into new realms with God but fear to step forward in full confidence and assurance into the unknown way."*

Isn't that well put! What I have seen as I have travelled extensively around the Body of Christ in the last few years is that there is a tension developing between the old and the new. With the emergence of the contemporary church and a new breed of younger apostolic leaders there has come a tension developing between the anchor men and the zealots, between the fathers and the fiery sons. And the question and the cry that has come to my heart at this stage is, "what is the balance?" How does God use this transition? What is He expecting from us?

In answer to these questions I have come to the conclusion that, <u>above all else</u>, God is expecting from us integrity. <u>God wants integrity in our hearts.</u>

2 Kings 2:2

> *"Then Elijah said to Elisha, 'stay here, for the Lord has sent me on to Bethel.' (Not a great deal of encouragement there.) And Elisha said, 'as the Lord lives and as your soul lives, I will not leave you,' so they went down to Bethel."*

Here we see one thing right from the outset of their relationship. <u>The commitment, the loyalty, and the perseverance of Elisha to stay with Elijah.</u> That is important.

2 Kings 2:3

> *"And the sons of the prophets who were at Bethel, the house of God, came out to Elisha and said to him 'Do you not know that the Lord will take away your master from over you today,' and he said, 'Yes I do know, keep silent.'"*

Who are these 'sons of the prophets'? Who do they represent to us today? I believe they are the coming generation; they are the emerging ministries of our day. As in this story they

"I will not leave you"

correctly discern what God's future intention is and they correctly discern that the Elijah era is about to close. With great enthusiasm they declare this to Elisha because he is the emerging era, obviously expecting his total and unqualified approval. Why? Because they had correctly discerned that Elisha was the incoming will of God and they are declaring that fact. They obviously think that he is going to be enthusiastic about his commendation of their great wisdom and understanding of the times. However, in one sentence he says two things which I believe God is trying to say to young men bursting forth in the ranks of leadership today. He declares two things that I believe are prophetically important, two things that are vital for us to understand if we are going to come through this transition as God intends us to.

The first one is that he confirms to them "Yes I know". He says, "Yes, your discernment of the times of God's intention is absolutely correct, God wants change, God wants a new era."

Then in his next statement he rebukes them for their over zealous impatience to see it happen. He says, "Yes I do know, you've discerned correctly enough, now will you keep silent." And it was a rebuke. Why? Because I believe that there was an attitude of ambition starting to creep through, that he had picked up. It was their intention to have more prominence in the new move than they had been able to have in the old move. And it was what Elisha had picked up. He also knew that if he allowed their impatience to touch his own heart unchallenged, it might well influence his own attitude toward Elijah.

2 Kings 2:4-5

> *"Then Elijah said to him, 'Elisha stay here please for the Lord has sent me on to Jericho' and he said, 'As the Lord lives and as your soul lives I will not leave you'. So they came to Jericho and the sons of the prophets who were at Jericho came to Elisha and said to him, 'Do you know that the Lord will take away your master from over you today'"*

Here they are at it again! "Don't you know it's a fresh move, don't you know God's finished with the old." He said, "Yes I know, will you keep silent."

2 Kings 2:6

> *"Then Elijah said to him, 'stay here please for the Lord has sent me on to Jordan' and he said, 'as the Lord lives, as your soul lives I will not leave you'. So the two of them went on together."*

Here we find, though he is stretched, though he is tested, the loyalty and the perseverance of Elisha remains totally unmovable. *"I will not leave you."* Loyalty and commitment really meant something to this man. Do you know why? Because he was a faithful man. He was not an ambitious man, he was not an arrogant man, he was not a self-seeking man, he was a selfless man and he was a man with a servant heart.

2 Kings 2:7

> *"And fifty men of the sons of the prophets went and stood facing them at a distance as the two of them stood by the Jordan."*

What does it mean *"they stood at a distance"*? It means, they were correctly discerning what was happening and in fact were eager to see it take place, yet they were not ready for Jordan. Jordan was a prophetic type of the coming cross of Calvary and has always spoken about the death to self, self-desire and self-ambition. In the Book of Joshua, as they prepared to go in and possess the land, Jordan became the point of no return, the moment of decision that demanded fundamental change. The self-will of the wilderness era had to be replaced with the discipline of coming under command and working together as a team without personal self-glory. Jordan was the place where they would have to die to their selfish desires, their ambitions for personal gain, their goals for glory and recognition. Jordan speaks of all of that.

"There are people in the Kingdom who are vulnerable to missing the hour of their visitation altogether because they are going too quickly, they are too impatient."

These "sons of the prophets" wanted a new move but they did not want it via the cross. It is true of many today. But God is not going to have this new move without His servants going to the cross because I believe God wants to birth a people in the image of His Son, the Servant King who walked in purity and power. He has no intention of settling for what is superficial or merely outwardly appealing.

146

The Pentecostal/Charismatic move has been powerful in its impact and achievement, with much having been accomplished for the Kingdom of God. However, it has also been riddled with contradiction and leaven and God is not about to do it again. God wants a move that is born out of the purity of His own heart's intention, and that means going to the cross first.

And so these zealots kept themselves somewhat at a distance when they realised that there was going to be a denial of self, when there was going to be a demand for brokenness and humility. The struggle between their spiritual expectations and their own humanity reflects exactly the experience of a lot of people who hover at such a place of decision at this present time. They want to please the Lord and to be fruitful in the kingdom but it is so hard to die to that sense of thrill that comes from the applause and the recognition. Sometimes the tug to be friends with the rich, the powerful, the globally impacting name, can be so strong that it puts into the shadows that former held simplicity of gaining ones identity out of being loved by Father and pleasing Him daily.

2 Kings 2:8

> *"Now Elijah took his mantle and he rolled it up and he*
> *struck the water and it was divided this way and that*
> *so that the two of them crossed over on dry ground."*

I want you to notice something which I believe is critical to this whole thing happening as God intends it to. It was the mantle of Elijah that was used to part the river Jordan, it wasn't Elisha's.

The mantle used was Elijah's. It was Elijah's authority that caused the final barrier to this fresh move of God to part before them and let them through, it was not Elisha's. The fact that it was Elijah's is most significant because if Elisha had listened to the sons of the prophets and had parted company with Elijah at either Bethel or Jericho (if impatience had won the day), then Elisha would have run ahead and arrived at Jordan and, to his horror, found that his mantle would have done nothing! Why? Because it was Elijah's mantle alone that was to part the Jordan and let him through. His own mantle would have been entirely insufficient for the task, he would have been ahead of schedule and he would have missed his hour of visitation.

We always talk about "missing it" as being something that is the result of people that are being too slow in following the vision (i.e. because they are too slow they miss the hour of their visitation).

Although this is undeniably true with many, there is the other extreme to consider also.

There are people in the Kingdom who are vulnerable to missing the hour of their visitation altogether because they are going too quickly, they are too impatient. It was essential that Elisha was still with Elijah at that moment, absolutely essential. You need to read 1 Kings 1:5-10 where Adonijah the son of Haggith exalted himself saying *"I will be king"*. Do you know that he correctly discerned that David's day was done? There was nothing wrong with his discernment but he had made an impatient move to see something happen. He wasn't a scoundrel, because it says that he was a good man and his father did not try to persuade him otherwise. Why? Because he trusted him, he was trustworthy, he was a good man! But he was impatient and his impatience not only brought havoc and tragedy to his own life, but to so many in Israel.

2 Kings 2:9

> *"And so it was when they had crossed over that Elijah said to Elisha, 'Ask what I may do for you before I am taken from you', and Elisha said to him, 'Please let a double portion of your spirit be upon me'."*

The subject of the double portion does well for our comment right now. The double portion speaks about the end time ministry that we all are craving and hungry for. When you take a look at the numbers of men in the Bible who were offered the double portion, you see a principle emerge. We find that Job was a man of the double portion, but look how he got it. David was a man of the double portion but look how he got it. <u>Trauma, testing, perseverance, trial of their integrity!</u>

We have already considered the difference between Saul and David in their anointing and how they became King. Saul was spied out, chosen, anointed, appointed and set in as King all in the space of one chapter – no work of the cross there. But look at his reign and look at his end. Powerful, great charisma, a deliverer of the people, he brought triumph and jubilation to God's people. He had them waving palm leaves and shouting in the street, he brought nothing but great glory to Israel. But he ended up taking advice from a witch!

"Younger emerging leaders today desperately need the ongoing wisdom and counsel of the 'fathers'"

You take a look at David. He's anointed by Samuel and then look what happened to him. He's got chapter after chapter of nothing but contradictions and heartache and the brokenness of the cross. But look at the king he became in contrast to Saul.

2 Kings 2:10

"So he said, 'you have asked a hard thing. Nevertheless if you see me when I am taken from you it shall be so for you, but if not it shall not be so'."

Right there Elisha could have blown it.

Elijah declared "If I'm not with you, if you're not within eyeball contact with me, if we are not still together when the moment happens, you won't be in it." And there are a lot of people today who in wanting to race out there with the new vision, adopt the attitude "who cares about the fathers, who cares about those who are a little bit slow on the uptake? Leave them in the dark; we've got a job to get done".

Quite obviously, I am speaking of some not all. It has been my great joy to see the love, honour and respect that many of our emerging leaders of the contemporary church still show towards the fathers that have passed the baton on to them. However, I still speak of a great number of visionary zealots, the new breed, and the emerging generation. To so many of them, the older more stable leaders are hindrances to the birthing of God.

But I believe the prophetic declaration of these verses is vital for them to understand. If the younger leaders are not still there, hand in hand with their older leaders when God births His final glorious visitation they simply won't be in it. It says quite clearly, "If you aren't with me when I am taken from you, you can't have it". I speak, of course, of the true fathers, not the Sauls. I speak of those whose hearts are soft and whose love for the Father is intimate and real. I speak of those who reach out to embrace the emerging Elisha company with the delight of true fathers who rejoice at seeing their children excel and go to heights they themselves were unable to climb.

Our younger emerging leaders today desperately need the ongoing wisdom and counsel of the "fathers" God has placed in the Church.

As I have considered the numbers of ministries that have become casualties in some way or simply ended up quitting in discouragement, I have come to the conclusion that the issue in common has been the lack of a "spiritual father" in their life. It is a genuine crisis in our age. It brings with it a lack of accountability and discipleship and ignores the undeniable thread of authority and submission that runs through New Testament Church life.

> *"Isolation breeds error. Let us never confuse freedom with independence."*

The argument is sometimes given that if one is in true fellowship with God and with Christian friends, that is accountability enough. This sounds spiritually right but it ignores one undeniable reality; our humanity, the gravitational pull towards independence and the asserting of our self-will.

In the beginning Adam and Eve enjoyed an awesome intimacy with God. They had the uninhibited love and friendship of a son and daughter with their Father due to the fact that there was no fear or apprehension in that relationship. Such negatives only came with the introduction of their self-will (sin). It was the asserting of their self-will that destroyed intimacy just as it does today, not only between us and the Father, but in marriages, friendships and every expression of relationship. In fact, that is where the degeneration of mankind began. It all started with a magnificent, delegated leader in the Angelic senior echelon stating "I will". If that is what self-will can do to an Arch Angel, just imagine what it can do to you and me.

In a pre-fallen world without the presence of our Adamic nature we would have lived life with a reverse gravitational pull - the default setting would have been set to gravitate upwards (Godward) instead of downwards (towards the base side of humanity). But the reality is that the fall did take place and today, even as in Paul's experience, we find there is an internal war between, *"the things I would, I do not and the things I would not do, I do"* (Romans 7:15).

The fact that you and I have an assured victory as we make the choice to stay intimate and submitted to Father and sensitive to the Holy Spirit's directives, is indisputable. Numerous are the scriptures that declare the Christ in us as far greater than the world and flesh.

However, the subtle and aggressive persuasion of our Adamic nature (self-will) should never be underestimated and it is foolishness and pride to do so. Here we come to the point. When one's self-will and fervency of desire becomes strong enough, it can colour how we read scriptures and how we "listen" to God. We read to confirm and we listen to confirm, not with a surrendered will. In most cases the intervention of friends then kicks in and they bring us back to seeing clearly.

But what if our human nature is so strong that we label them all as simply "out of tune"? What then? If none of them has an established and recognised authority role in our lives, we simply do not have to listen to them. But if we do have established clear authority figures in our lives (that our spouse and immediate friends all know about) then there is a recognised "Court of Appeal". The fact that you have been the one, in a time of greater spiritual clarity, to establish that figure (or eldership team) just might be enough added weight to swing you back from the error you were so resolved to embrace.

Friends we need such figures in our lives. If there is one indisputable principle, it is that "isolation breeds error".

Let us never confuse true freedom with independence. Independence is, in fact, handing over your freedom to the tyranny of your corrupted human nature. True freedom is to be under authority but under an authority that is so liberating, empowering and releasing that its inclusion in your life becomes the instrument of your greater potential being realised. All God-given authority figures in our lives should produce:

1. greater intimacy with Father
2. a greater sense of personal freedom and boldness in our Christian walk
3. a greater release of our gifting and calling
4. a greater sense of fulfillment and fruitfulness
5. a greater sense of God-directed destiny in our lives
6. greater evidence of Godly character and true discipleship

There are those who say that all structure of authority in the Church is wrong, man made and controlling. Not only is this Biblically wrong but practically wrong as well. True authority empowers the authority of the one submitted to it.

In most cases that authority figure will be your local church pastor, but in the case of a senior minister it would be an apostolic father figure. However, where that individual is themselves an apostolic leader, it may well be a corporate authority such as a "Board", "Eldership" or a number of peer Apostolic leaders who are clearly established as such.

Many would disagree with this and point to issues such as pride, financial corruption or moral failure in certain senior leaders. However, if the true nature of apostolic authority and the transparency and accountability that it brings is understood, then such issues are only able to conceive and grow in an environment in which one is not subject to accountability.

Although we were created originally in Adam to relate directly to God alone for spiritual accountability, since the Fall it has been necessary to introduce human accountability. We all know of the abuse of this and we have all heard the cries of those who wish to retain their independence of will, that such philosophy opens the door to papacy and a rejection of the priesthood of every Believer. I do not deny that such abuse has taken place but the answer is not to throw out the Biblical truth because of it. Since we all now wrestle with the fallen human nature that can be so subtle and convincing when wanting its own way. God places those around us who see us more clearly than we can see ourselves at such times. Our humanity is still too much alive for us to do life successfully on our own and without the protection that such transparency and submission brings.

Some emerging ministers will say that they have such accountability with their peers or their local eldership. Although I strongly encourage those relationships and they are absolutely vital, they do not replace the need for the "Centurion Principle" in our lives. Let me explain that.

"Jesus grew in authority because he was under the authority of His Father"

In Luke chapter seven a Roman Centurion sends word to Jesus that his servant is sick and requests a healing word from Jesus to be sent, explaining that Jesus Himself would not need to come as he recognizes the authority under which Jesus lived His life.

Luke 7:8, 9

> *"For I also am a man set under authority, having under me soldiers. And I say to one, Go, and he goes; and to another, Come, and he comes; and to my servant, Do this, and he does it.*
>
> *And hearing these things, Jesus marvelled at him. And turning to the crowd following Him, He said, I say to you, I have not found such faith, no, not in all Israel."*

Jesus marvelled at the Centurion's perception of a fundamental law of the Kingdom. That whose authority you are under determines the level of authority in your own life. The degree to which you are under authority, to that degree do you have authority. It also determines the nature or "character" of the authority you express. It is simply not possible to grow into a greater Kingdom authority if those you are "submitted" to, are of less or even similar authority than you presently walk in.

"A 'father' is more interested in who you are"

Jesus grew in authority because he was under the authority of His Father. The Centurion grew in his authority because he was under the authority of Caesar. It is a fundamental law. Submission for the purpose of discipleship is to those who have greater authority than our own.

You can however be in submission in your attitude to your peers or those under you (as in a senior minister submitting to their eldership) and this is healthy and vitally necessary. I believe in the value of team and the need for a leader to submit to the collective wisdom of those ordained to be his/her checks and balances. Humility demands it. However, say a senior leader is subject to an eldership's spiritual authority in matters of personal spiritual growth and development (and there is no other more senior authority to look to) the growth of that senior leader will be restrained to the level of that eldership. Instead of providing the example for the elders to follow, he/she ends up following their example and the leader becomes the one being led. Of course, in some cases, the "father" figure may be one of the elders but not because of their eldership office. They are such because of a relationship that God has forged between the two individuals that provides the personal accountability of which we have spoken.

When Margaret and I relinquished the local church leadership in order to minister itinerant, I handed the baton to Jim Shaw and he replaced me as the senior minister. For the following five years I remained in that local church. In all matters concerning the policy and government of that local church I was submitted to Jim's decisions and he was submitted to the collective wisdom of his eldership. However, then and now, Jim has remained a son-in-the-Lord to me and recognizes me as his Apostolic father figure. It is a wonderful relationship (that extends to his wife, Anneke) and it is also mutually enriching. I gain so much from observing those two people and their walk with Jesus. But, because it is a relationship, I am and will always be, "dad".

It is tragic that there has been such an abuse of authority in the past that we now are often filled with apprehension when considering this element of apostolic fatherhood in our own lives. The vulnerability of it should not intimidate us but it must bring in to focus the need for certain non-negotiable attributes when looking for such a person.

Do they have the evidence of an intimate relationship with God in prayer? Do they have a spirit of humility and servanthood? Do they have good credibility and acceptance with other senior ministries? Does their own track record fill you with confidence in their wisdom? Do they genuinely love you as a person rather than see you only through the eyes of what you can achieve?

A mentor is more interested in what you do, whereas a father is more interested in who you are. Paul said *"you have many instructors (mentors) but not many fathers"* (1 Corinthians 4:15).

One of the more notable expectations of the last chapter in Church and World history is *"the turning of the hearts of the children to the fathers and the hearts of the fathers to their children"* (Malachi 4:6). We must believe that this generation that has had such a lack of fatherhood in the natural will now discover the releasing empowerment of it in the life of the Church. No one disputes that it is God alone who is ultimately both Father and final authority in our lives, but our attitude towards Him is most often reflected by our attitude towards those of a human form that He has placed into our lives.

One last comment on this. What of those who have come to a stage of life in which their parents have been removed? I am now a grandfather (61 years old as I write this) and the list of those older than I and still serving the Lord fervently grows shorter each year. Men and women like our beloved Kevin & Rene Conner (true examples of "fatherhood" who are a constant inspiration to me) are less and less easy to find. In addition to this, we have the tragedy of so many of my generation placing their trust in an apostolic figure who ended up corrupted in some manner which demanded a discontinuing of ones submission to them.

When one by virtue of age, years of walking with God or the loss of their previous apostolic relationship, becomes a "patriarch" figure they may no longer be able to point to a clear cut spiritual father/mother in their lives. This is where the attitude of humility will allow God to bring into their lives wonderful men and women of God to provide that wisdom and accountability. I enjoy that relationship with my wife, Margaret and my Board who are all well respected senior members of the Body of Christ. I have also given other apostolic men and women the right to speak into my life and hold me accountable and these are known to my wife and to my ministry team at DMM. I also recognise the wonderful spiritual leadership of Mark Conner, the senior minister in CityLife Church, my local church where I have been committed for the last seventeen years since coming to Australia.

So the message is that if one has the attitude and heart for it, God will always supply these wonderful people in our lives and none of us are exempt from the need of them.

It is only right to assume that the powerful mantle that came upon Elisha was due in no small part to his relationship with Elijah as his God-given father figure. I fervently believe that today's generation of emerging ministers, if possessing that Elisha attitude, can also come to know the increased empowerment that such a relationship can bring.

REFLECTION

There is so much in the Elijah/Elisha story. You may be an Elijah who has ministered for some time now or you may be an emerging Elisha. As we reflect on this story, ask yourself the following questions.

1. How is my loyalty?

2. How is my discernment?

3. How is my patience?

4. How is my influence on others?

5. Am I serving faithfully where I am right now?

6. Do I want to see a new move of God?

7. When the new day comes, do I hold on to yesterday or do I move forward positively?

8. How is my respect for the spiritual 'fathers/mothers' in my life? In what ways do I honour them?

PRAYER

Father, when transition time comes, and I know it will someday, I pray that I will deal with it like Elisha did. Help me to always honour the spiritual fathers and mothers. Help me to embrace change positively through the cross. Lord I want to move when you direct, not too slow and not too fast. I need Your wisdom and I need Your patience. Father I pray that You will speak to me more on this issue over the next few days as I take time to meditate on it.

Chapter Twelve

COST

of the

DOUBLE

PORTION

There is a cry for the double portion, a cry of the Church for greater works, the restoration of the book of Acts. But far more than that we need to see a restoration of Biblical authority, Biblical structure and the recognition of the ministries that will release such a visitation.

It is my conviction that the apostles and prophets God is raising up around the face of the globe will be broken vessels, men and women of humility who know what it is for their own humanity and frailty to have to go again and again to the cross. They will also be people who exalt the King and His Kingdom above the confines of their own denominations. They are going to be right across the board and they are going to be as at home in an Apostolic church as they are in a Baptist church, as they are in an Assemblies of God church, as they are in whatever church you want to put a tag on. They are going to be at home in the Body and the Body is going to be at home with them. Why? Because there is something about the fragrance of Jesus out of a broken vessel that doesn't have any barriers and God wants to restore such vessels to be the instruments of His grace in this hour.

What the King says to many people today is, "if you can see me when I appear to be taken from you, you can have it". If you can still see the King, if you can still love Him, if you can still worship Him, if you can still hold fast to your integrity when He appears to be taken from you; you will experience a depth of trust not gained at any other time. When you feel like your prayers are bouncing off the ceiling, when you feel like you are devoid of any contact with Him and yet you hold fast your integrity, you keep your confession one of adoration and submission to His intention, God is digging a well of compassion and identification within you that prepares you to be touched with the pain of others. If you can acknowledge Him when He appears to be taken from you, your faith becomes anchored in deep convictions of Biblical truth rather than the fleeting and superficial evidences of blessing that so many seem to rely on today.

That is the price of the double portion. A relationship with God which has been forged like fine steel to become an instrument that God knows will not buckle in the days of conflict ahead. God has seen a vessel to whom he can entrust the power and dominion of His Kingdom authority and will not be corrupted in the process. The "double portion" principle in scripture belongs to those who have been through the fire but do not smell of smoke. It belongs to those who have kept their hearts without guile and their confession free of accusation towards God and their brethren.

The classic example is Job. But Moses, David and many others also give testimony to this truth. So maybe what's happening to some of you right now is not a negative after all. It may not be a cancellation of God's call, but rather a stepping stone in the process of its greater fulfilment.

2 Kings 2:11

> *"Then it happened as they continued on and talked
> that suddenly a chariot of fire appeared with the horses
> of fire and separated the two of them and Elijah went
> up by a whirlwind into heaven."*

Elijah is gone, the era is no more and the chapter is closed. But friends please notice that it was not because of Elisha.

God's intention has indeed been realised but it was not because of Elisha and it was not because of the sons of the prophets. It was because of the sovereign intervention of the Lord. God did it! I want you to understand this. Realise the importance of it because for the next year, and the year after that, and the year after that, Elisha would have had an assurance of heart, gained from knowing that he did not make it happen, God did it.

"A coup from beneath is never right"

There is nothing as insecure, there is nothing that will make a man so vulnerable to the attacks of hell and undermine whatever good he may be doing, than to know that he, by his own hints and scheming, brought about what he is doing, rather than God.

Friends, I want to know, if I am going out into scary new territory, that it is God who put me there. I want to know that God has sovereignly ordained it, sovereignly appointed it and that I simply was a piece of clay in His hand and did what I was told. If I have any suspicion that any manipulative powers in me arranged the situation, then I am vulnerable to doubt for the rest of my life and the devil, my adversary, will well know it.

Elisha did nothing to hasten Elijah's end, he did everything to try and prevent it because of his integrity. He said, "I will never leave you," and in so doing released the situation and timing so that God could sovereignly do it.

Let me say it most bluntly. A coup from beneath is never right.

Let us put it in a local church setting. Division and the splitting of a church congregation, simply to fulfil a person's desire for their own ministry promotion is never right. A true servant, a lover of people, would never knowingly cause such heartache and disrepute to the Lord's people.

When a David allows impatience and the pressure of circumstances to pressure him to that end, he pays a terrible price. In the process, David dies and Saul is born. Impatience gives way to self-will and self-will hardens the heart to the Holy Spirit's pleadings from within. The ultimate outcome is a deceived heart. Believing that what they are doing is now right and they do so with such convincing zeal and fervour that many around them are rallied to the cause. Sauls are only Davids that fight their Sauls. Think about that.

The fact that most of the people feel them to be right and most of the circumstances indicate they are right, means absolutely nothing. The principles of humility, integrity and servanthood say they are not right. The examples of scripture say they are not right. Our *"greater than Solomon"* (Matthew 12:42) will test the hearts of emerging leadership to find the heart of the true "mother". The one whose love for the people, submission to God's sovereignty and embracing of the cross within, all cry out with such strength that they would rather lose all than divide God's people.

Quite obviously, however, there are times when a Saul does need to be removed from their position. There are times when the sin or manipulation of people is proven and the protection or rescue of God's people is the paramount concern. However, how this is achieved is the vital issue. It can never be by a "coup" or a "split-the-church" policy. First, the Eldership should gather with the senior person and reason and counsel with them, pointing out the scriptural demands of character. Should there be a hardening of their Saulish resolve, then this is the time to bring in senior leaders of the Body of Christ, those who have recognised apostolic oversight with that local congregation.

For this reason, an Eldership should know who such senior leaders are. This provides a security to them and the congregation and accountability to the senior person also. With many independent Churches today, wonderfully raised up by a strong apostolic leader, there is an even greater need for churches to know to whom they can appeal should there come a non-resolvable contention between the eldership and the senior minister.

Having said this, let me emphasise that the circumstances would have to be most serious and the leader unrepentant, for such steps to be taken.

Coming back to the response of the younger leader to their senior leader who appears to be "losing it". I was faced with that decision myself years ago and God spoke to me very clearly about it. Sauls are only Davids that end up fighting their Sauls in order to try and work out God's will in their own way. Impatience!

Although you can't really liken Saul to Elijah for they were totally different, there is one principle that remains the same. David would have served Saul to the day he died. The breach between David and Saul was not of David's making, it was Saul's choice. Even though Saul had hunted David in caves and thrown spears at him, if Saul had wanted a reconciliation of heart to heart relationship with David, David would have accepted it and been back at his side within a moments notice. He never lost his love for him; he never lost his desire to serve him as the Lord's anointed. If he could do it with someone like Saul, how much easier it must have been for someone like Elisha to do with Elijah. Yet many an impatient Elisha today has treated their older leader more as a Saul than an Elijah.

2 Kings 2:12

> *"Now Elisha saw it and he cried out, 'My father, my father the chariot of Israel and the horsemen,' so he saw him no more and he took hold of his own clothing and he tore them into two pieces."*

Notice the reference, *"My father, my father"*. Even then there remains recognition; even then there is still the cry of his heart towards his father, his apostolic covering, his headship till the end.

The second thing to notice here in verse 12 is that he took hold of his own clothes, his existing clothes, and tore them into two pieces. This is the final phase of the transition.

The time had come and God had birthed the new era by His own hand and in His own timing. Reluctance had to go. This now was the timing of God and it was time for a bold new initiative. With a tearing and renting of the old garments, Elisha puts himself into the position of no turning back. He has no option but to clothe himself with a fresh mantle and that is the mantle of the double portion. This is indeed the other side of the coin. It is a message to the older leaders, the fathers and mothers of past and present moves. There has to come a letting go in order for there to be an embracing.

164

Elisha had worn those garments a long time, they were comfortable and familiar and there is a certain sense of security about the familiar. But it is a false security that restricts one from walking that life of faith and obedience which constantly demands we step out into fresh and unfamiliar territory.

Let me ask you a question. How many want to walk on water? Who wouldn't?! Right? But, it's not about how many want to walk on water; it's about how many want to get out of the boat (even for us Irish that is profound). You can't walk on water unless you get out of the boat! We all want the miraculous testimony of how God's faithfulness came through but not too many of us by choice would put ourselves in the position where we would need that miracle in the first place. Friends, we have to be able to let go of the old securities in order to present ourselves as candidates for God's fresh chapter in our lives.

1 Samuel 23:16-18 is the story of Jonathan making covenant with David.

> *"And Jonathan, Saul's son, arose and went to David into the woods, and strengthened his hand in God.*
>
> *And he said to him, 'Do not fear, for the hand of Saul my father shall not find you. And you shall be king over Israel, and I shall be next to you. And my father Saul knows that also'.*
>
> *And the two of them cut a covenant before Jehovah. And David stayed in the forest, and Jonathan went to his house."*

There is a tremendous warning in this scripture because Jonathan speaks to us about the average person right now who sees the waning of the old and the coming of the new. There are a lot of people today who are perplexed over the presenting of that choice. But let me say, that when it has been God who has done it, and when the hour of choice is presented to us; let us not be like Jonathan. When God is challenging you in your spirit and in your heart to take some steps in God and to let go of the old and to embrace the new, then do it!

Jonathan saw the anointing, he loved the anointing, he appreciated the anointing, he risked his life for the anointing, he even made covenant and said to the anointed, *"you will reign and I will only be second to you"*. He couldn't have done more to prove his total acceptance of David and yet the tragedy is that he doesn't rule and reign with David but dies with Saul. Why? Because he failed to make the transition complete. His noble but misguided loyalty to the past had him positioned in the wrong place at the wrong time.

Some will ask was he not showing respect for his father by staying? Was he not doing the very thing that you have been talking about and continuing to serve the existing leader? At an initial glance, this is exactly what it appears to be and may well have been the reality of Jonathan's heart at that time. However, it brings to our attention a vital consideration – an individual's responsibility to follow truth and pursue God's intention and yet still hold to the law of integrity.

I have said that a coup from beneath is never right and this is true. But this should not indicate to any that it is right to stay under the authority of one who has clearly departed from God's heart and His ways. With the understanding that one in authority imparts into the life of those under that authority, we must realise that whose authority we are under determines the nature of our own development and growth. It is betrayal of God's intention for us to allow the life and ministry that he has given into our care to be corrupted and defiled by one whose impartation to us is impure. It is also wrong that we continue to submit to a leader whose theology is now substantially different to our own. Such misguided loyalty can only result in either compromise of our own biblical convictions or our usurping of that leader's authority by our conversations with others concerning our points of disagreement. Neither option is ideal and will ultimately breed contention.

In such an environment one is faced with the making of a difficult but vital decision – to leave, but to do so with integrity and grace. Go to your leader and explain the points of disagreement with a gracious spirit. Should that conversation not see a closing of the gap, then share the *"do two walk together unless they are agreed"* (Amos 3:3) principle with them and advise that you are leaving but will do so with the utmost integrity. You will not bad mouth them as a leader, you will not entice others to join you, and you will not start up another church in competition a hundred metres down the road.

By handling the exit with integrity you keep open the bridge to that leader's heart and minimise the potential for a harsh reaction and further distress to both parties.

The bottom line is that we must continue to grow and develop into the image of Christ and fulfil His calling in our lives. This will demand that we embrace change and be willing for such times of transition when they are forced upon us. Change is critical for one's destiny to be realised. If the authority we are under has a heart for God and is soft towards change themselves, then our continued loyalty and service should be fervent. But if that leader hardens their heart and increasingly gives evidence of the "Saul" within, then the above challenge must be responded to positively. The one thing that is not in question is that we must continue to have a heart for change and inner growth.

Psalm 55:19

> *"Because they have no changes therefore they do not fear God."*

The evidence of His Lordship in us is not that we pay our tithe. The evidence of His Lordship in us is not that we read the Bible. The evidence of His Lordship in us is not that we pray. The evidence of His Lordship in us is not that we go to church. There is only one evidence of true Lordship in our lives and that is change. If He is Lord, we change. If we are not changing friends, then he is not Lord.

Having said all of that, I must again emphasise that such situations are the rare exception, not the rule. In the vast majority of cases, the father figure that God gives us will be one in love with God and God's intention. The fact that they are from an earlier generation does not diminish their effectiveness as our Apostolic input but greatly enhances it. It is their accumulated wisdom and understanding of God that is critical to the birthing process of God's call in your own life.

2 Kings 2:13

> *"He also took up the mantle of Elijah that had fallen from him and went back and stood by the bank of the Jordan."*

Wouldn't you think it would have been just a little bit of a tragedy now if Elisha had been there ahead of time or got separated somehow from Elijah?

If he hadn't been there, then firstly he couldn't have crossed Jordan on his own, and secondly there would have been no mantle to pick up.

2 Kings 2:13-14

> *"So he also took the mantle that had fallen from him, went back and stood by the bank of Jordan. Then he took the mantle of Elijah that had fallen from him and struck the water and said, 'where is the Lord God of Elijah?' when he also struck the water it divided this way and that and Elisha crossed over."*

Note he says *"Lord God of Elijah"*. Still there is that honouring, still there is that respect, still there is that recognition of his father's ministry, it doesn't ever leave him.

2 Kings 2:16-18

> *"Then they said to him, 'look now there are fifty strong men with your servants please let them go and search for your master lest perhaps the spirit of the Lord has taken him up and cast him upon some mountain.' And he said, 'you shall not send anyone,' but when they urged him till he was ashamed, he said, 'send them out'. Therefore they sent fifty men and they searched*

for three days but they could not find him and when they came to him for he had stayed in Jericho he said, 'did I not say to you do not go?'"

Wasted time and energy trying to hang onto the old. Correctly discerning the times, knowing what was going to happen but when God actually starts to do it, they react the opposite way. They say, "Oh God, what about our sentimentalities? We've got to find him; we've got to bring him back right now." So they spent all their time and energy trying to rediscover him and bring him back. And God says, "What is done is done, we're today now, we're not yesterday, it's time to move on."

Elisha understood the process, he understood the transition. He understood that for the new season to be fully entered into, the season wherein the double portion of Elijah would be expressed in his own life, Elisha would need to move on.

Isaiah 43:18-19 says

"remember not the former days neither consider the things of old for behold now I do a new thing."

Elisha knew that the double portion carried a cost. It carried with it an essential condition. There was a process of transition that if ever aborted, the double portion would be lost. Elisha understood that it was his attitude towards Elijah and his honouring of God through the process of transition, no matter where that would take him, that would determine whether or not he would receive the double portion.

It is the same for us today, as young leaders look toward the future and as the time for transition from the old to the new comes to hand. For a release of the new to be doubly empowered, for the leaders of tomorrow to truly take on the double portion, that same process, of transition must take place.

An incorruptible heart is able to make the transition from the old to the new with honour and integrity.

REFLECTION

1. Are you a leader now faced with handing on the baton? Have you taken time to consider the passing of your ministry to another that will empower them to see many times the fruit that you saw? What is the process that Father is laying out for you to embrace so as to empower the next generation?

2. Are you a leader entering into a time of transition from your ministry of yesterday to your ministry of tomorrow? What is the process that Father is laying out for you to embrace that will empower your future ministry?

3. Have you taken time to consider how you will honour your Elijah figure?

PRAYER

Father, please forgive me for times when I have sought my own ends, my own promotion, to preserve my own legacy. I need you to guide me through the moments in my life of transition. Help me to honour those that have gone before, and help me to empower those that are yet to come. I trust your purposes, and I submit my will to whatever part you would have me play in your Kingdom. I love you Lord, and I love your people.

Chapter Thirteen

Let INTEGRITY GUIDE YOU

What causes transitions to fail? Why do we not see successive double portion's being handed down from generation to generation? What aborts the empowering process in a transition?

Look at 2 Kings 2:16-19. This passage is particularly important; in fact it ties together all that I have been saying in the previous chapter.

The men of the city said to Elisha in verse 19, *"Please notice the situation of the city is pleasant, as my lord sees the city is pleasant but the water is bad and the ground is barren."*

When I read this something about the verse just ripped into my spirit and I said, "God what are you trying to tell me here?" And so I looked up the Hebrew on the word "barren". It literally means, "that which causes miscarriage". I suddenly realised that God was trying to say something to my heart. What causes spiritual miscarriage? We are on the brink of a beautiful new day, a glorious new birth in the Body of Christ but it is threatened right now in many quarters. What causes miscarriages?

Why would a miscarriage take place in the Body of Christ when the pregnant expectancy is born of God, totally conceived by the Holy Spirit? What is it that would cause a miscarriage? What is it that threatens this fresh move of God right now? Is it doctrines? No. Is it structure? No.

I had a pastor ring me up and he was talking to me about his particular denomination, which was an evangelical one. His own fellowship was becoming more and more charismatic and he said, "I can no longer work because the denominational structure will not allow me to". As he was saying this, something was going off in my heart and I started asking him questions, "Are you allowed to do this? Well yes. Are you allowed to do that? Well yes. Are you allowed to do that? Well yes." I suddenly realised that it was not the structure that was holding the man down.

> *"Attitudes and motivations of the heart cause (spiritual) miscarriages"*

How about philosophy of leadership? No, even that doesn't cause it. I was in a certain situation with senior leaders of a denomination that will remain nameless. Two groups of people were sitting down with two different philosophies of leadership and I looked at these two groups of men. On one hand, I had those whose definition of leadership and understanding of structure was entirely different to mine and on the other hand, I had a group who were completely in accordance with what I felt God was really trying to say. The latter group was discerning correctly what God was saying and I felt the first group were a little reluctant about it all, which was understandable. However, tension was rising and strain was developing. Who was right, who was God wishing to confirm?

When I prayed about it, I was amazed at God's answer. It is not the structure, not leadership style or the doctrine that cause miscarriages.

*Attitudes and motivations of the heart cause miscarriages.

You see there is only one thing that causes spiritual miscarriage folks, and that is sin. *The sin of wrong attitudes causes spiritual miscarriages.

On one side of the tension you have the attitudes of rigidity, inflexibility, lack of genuine hunger, stubbornness, a desire to hang on to the old at any cost. There are those who can be a part of a denominational family and be free in their spirits and there are those to whom the family means more than the Body of Christ or anything else. They are rigid in that which has been their thing and their revelation and their doctrine and their denomination and those attitudes of rigidity withstand what God is trying to say and do.

But on the other hand, you have attitudes of impatience, frustration, insensitivity and spiritual pride. When one's maturity has not kept pace with one's revelation; when one's humility and servanthood is eclipsed by one's zeal to see it happen now!

The answer to all these conflicting attitudes and responses is found in:

Proverbs 11:2-3

> *"The integrity of the upright will guide them."*

How do you know what choice to make? How do you know what decision to make? How do you know where the balance is? Listen to integrity. He speaks from within by the Holy Spirit. Ask yourself if your attitude and response delights the heart of God or offends Him. The critical issue in relation to God's acceptance or rejection of your actions is the attitudes you hold.

I have heard so many definitions of Integrity. My own goes like this

Integrity :

"Purity of thought, motivation, intention, attitude and speech."

Integrity is that quality the Psalmist cried out for in Psalm 51:6 when he correctly observes of the Lord *"You desire truth in the inward parts"*. The word for "truth" is also able to be translated "transparency". Our "inward parts" is the realm of our motivations and attitudes. God wants men and women who are pure, transparent, totally honest and completely honourable in the secret world of their thoughts from where their speech and actions will originate.

It was also the cry of Job. Even after having been tested so sorely, we find his cry in Job 31:6 *"Let me be weighed in a just balance that God may know my integrity"*. His cry was heard and his cry was rewarded. The integrity of Job held firm, and as a result, we find yet again that the contradictions were not a cancellation of the call but rather a process to see it fulfilled. The price of the double portion. Through such trauma there would emerge a whole new man. One who had undergone the deep dealings of God. A man who God could entrust with twice the mantle, twice the authority, twice the impact on the society he had known previously.

But what of those who had misjudged him?

Those who had known none of the contradictions, those who it had appeared God was blessing all the time that Job was in such trouble?

I call them the "high-flyers of the bless me circuit". They had all the apparent success but lacked integrity of speech.

In Job 42:7, 8 we see their judgement. The humbling of having to go to the very one they have criticised for their desperate need of God's forgiveness. It simply was their turn for the work of the cross to be brought to bear.

In Psalm 41:11, 12 David rejoices that his enemy has not been able to triumph over him. Yet he had known betrayal, pain, anguish, and his own sons returning his love with treachery. How then, does he make such a claim?

David knew that the greatest enemy of all was his own humanity!

The desire to fight back; the desire to trade blow for blow; the temptation to lay aside the disciplines of integrity. The consideration of "his rights" as King; the pressure to use his office to hit back. Such emotions, David knew, were the real enemy. But with Saul, with Absalom and with Adonijah David was able to say: *"my enemy, my self-will, my carnality, has not triumphed over me... You have upheld me in my integrity"* (see Psalms 41:12).

His shout of joy was that the integrity of God in him had triumphed! This can be your confession too. This can be the hallmark of your life. This can be true for you as it was true for King David.

Let me quote in full Proverbs 11:2

> *"When pride comes, then comes shame; but with the humble is wisdom. The integrity of the upright will guide them, but the perversity (lack of integrity) of the unfaithful will destroy them."*

Again I say, let integrity guide you from within. Integrity will speak!

Integrity will always take the way of the cross
Integrity will lay down his rights rather than pick them up
Integrity would rather lose money than lose honesty
Integrity will protect rather than expose
Integrity will support rather than undermine
Integrity will unite rather than divide
Integrity does not seek its own, but rather the good of others
Integrity is selfless not selfish
Integrity cares more about the reputation of God than the furtherance of its own cause or ministry

We must ask ourselves the question, what would integrity tell us in the situation?

Let integrity guide you!

Our Confidence

With so many questions and unexplained events in the world right now, how can we know peace and confidence in the steps we take toward the future?

"The integrity of the upright will guide them. Proverbs 11:2-3"

Job 4:6 gives the answer

"Is not your reverence (awe of God) your confidence? And the integrity of your ways, your hope?"

* Our confidence in our future is not that we are called or gifted. It is in that we have walked in integrity; we have lived in humility and transparency before God and man.

The reason why Joseph did not despair in prison was that he knew he had kept his integrity. The reason why David did not despair in Adullum's Cave was that he knew he had kept his integrity.

The unassailable peace in knowing we have wronged no man in our mind or heart! The King of the Church is allowing a time of travail and fresh scrutiny of His people. There is shaking and controversy; perplexities and unexplainable events.

Why? Because it is in the midst of controversy that the true hearts of people are made known today. And through the grey shade of the humanity which blankets the Church, integrity will arise to shine with the brilliance of a new hope!

Finally here, let me quote to you Titus 2:6-8

> *"Likewise exhort the young men to be sober minded, in all things showing yourself to be a pattern of good works; in doctrine showing integrity, reverence (Godly awe) incorruptibility, sound speech that cannot be condemned, that one who is an opponent may be ashamed, having nothing evil to say of you."*

Can you imagine the frustration of Satan's hellish legions? No matter what they hurl at them – love of money, lust of the eye, public acclaim, disappointment, jealousy, grievances, wounds of a brother. To no avail! The report each woeful little demon has to return with is the same "this one is incorruptible! We cannot break their integrity!"

What a glorious declaration! This is the incorruptible heart! This is what we are called to as disciples of Christ if we are to represent Him accurately. It is the goal to which the Holy Spirit is totally committed to empower.

What a fitting offering of our hearts back to the Saviour. What pleasure it must bring to His heavenly courts.

Friends, if it is your heart's desire, then let me assure you again. In the full surrender of your heart and will to His, integrity will guide you.

REFLECTION

1. Have you seen the integrity of your heart triumph through times of contradiction and trial?

2. If not what would you have done differently?

3. Think about a challenging situation you might be facing right now. What would integrity tell you to do?

4. Now that you've thought about what integrity would do, are you going to do it? Are you going to care more about the reputation of Christ or your own 'right'?

PRAYER

Father my integrity is one of the most important things in my life. I can think of times when I have reacted in a way that has contradicted what I know integrity would do. For these times, please forgive me. If there are people I need to put things right with, please make it clear to me and give me the strength to follow through. For the future, I ask that You will help me to live a life of integrity that flows easily from my love for you, a life based on the quest to more accurately represent you in all that I do.

_____ *Chapter Fourteen* _____

GOD'S
SELECTION

We are all in a time of transition. A time when God's trumpet heralds a new day dawning. A day of the "Davids". A day when the "Sauls" will be revealed for who they are.

The question arises. Is it too late for them? Will God discard such strong leaders of yesterday and allow only those younger men, born of this present move, to take up the sceptre? No!

It is true that many are reluctant of the changes that are necessary. It is true that many will disqualify themselves. It is true that not all will allow the Lord's sovereign will to prevail. There will be tragedies; the one's for whom we shall weep. However, we must not judge them too quickly. We must endeavour to understand the reality of their fear and pray them through.

It is also true that many "Sauls" today are passing through their Gethsemane, coming to the foot of the cross, and in their brokenness, experiencing the death of that which they have known. From that death, the Lord is resurrecting many to serve Him and His people with renewed commission. Not only is this possible, it's vital! We must believe for it, pray for it, and earnestly contend for it.

If out of the ashes of dead Sauls, the Lord can grant us the ministry of older, more experienced Davids, then this present zeal of fire can be tempered by the grace and stability of their wisdom.

Without them and the testimony of their pain and brokenness, there may well be the tragedy of some of today's "Davids" becoming vulnerable to the very spirit of Saul that they themselves have so vigorously rejected in others.

The answer is not for us to set ourselves up as Pharisaic judges nor to assume that we have the necessary wisdom to do such. We must love one another, genuinely care for one another, and be vigilant in selfless prayer for those whom we suspect are finding the road from Saul more difficult to take.

Above all, we must have that life transforming encounter for ourselves, daily living in that place of His intimacy, keeping the reality of the cross forever in view as we evaluate what He is doing through our lives. For it is only then that our example of the true Christ nature may be seen as a light of hope and conviction to those who even now are sensing the challenge of this their hour of transition.

"God was looking for a man with the right heart"

✱ Let us always keep before us the understanding that ours is an authority of privilege, not of right, and that its objective is not the extension of our ministry, but the extensions of His Kingdom, in and through His people.

In 1 Samuel 16:6-13 the selection of God is worthy of note for it still applies today. Note verse 6 and 7.

> *"So it was, when they came, that he looked at Eliab and said, 'Surely the Lord's anointed is before Him'. But the Lord said to Samuel, 'Do not look at his appearance or at the height of his stature, because I have refused him. For the Lord does not see as man sees; for man looks at the outward appearance, but the Lord looks at the heart.'"*

The selection was no longer to be on the basis of prowess (in stature or in gift) as with the selection of Saul. No! Now the selection was the least likely, the youngest. Though the last by human choice, David was God's selection for one reason; the condition of his heart.

✱ God was looking for a man with the right heart.

No longer looking for greatness of stature, He was looking for greatness of integrity, devotion and humility. He was looking for the heart of a shepherd that would be large enough to receive the pain and needs of his flock, Israel.

He was looking for a worshipper whose life and love was the pleasing of His heart; yet a warrior who without fear would lay down his life for the sheep when challenged by the lion and bear.

It is not that Saul was entirely evil, nor David entirely good.

Both were mortal men who could have well identified with the Paul of Romans chapter 7. Both had the reality of their humanity, the presence of their own will.

Yet for one, the pleasure of God was optional and for the other, a driving passion. For one, self was the most valid of considerations and for the other, a repugnant enemy to be denied.

Both had the reality of choice:

- One chose to take, the other to give.
- One chose to resent, the other to love.
- One chose to dominate, the other to serve.
- One chose to establish his own kingdom and lost it, the other to lay it down and not only was granted it, but with it he gained an even higher prize; intimate communion with God.

David was just a young man, the youngest of them all. Not much at all in the eyes of man. But what a heart toward God, what abandonment of will to serve Him!

God's hand is upon such today. Davids are emerging.

"They are identified by their incorruptible heart"

They are men and women with gentle hearts toward people, yet fierce, faith-filled indignation toward the legions of hell. Worshipping warriors for whom the necessary recognition is a burden allowed with reluctance. Their ambition is not the shallow acclaim of mortal man but the eternal commendation of the King they love!

They are emerging in the church, the market place, politics and sport. They are His Church Triumphant which has the gratitude of the redeemed and the passion of the called. They are those whose hearts bear the stamp of a John Wesley or a Billy Graham, yet are uniquely creative and suited to our contemporary world.

There is something about them that inspires you to believe and challenges you to become. They have made excellence a quest and denied humanity's persistent call to mediocrity. They radiate His life like a magnet of reawakened hope to the sceptic and a reassurance to the discouraged.

They are not identified by age or background, gifting or experience. They are not identified by race or culture, denomination or connections. They are not identified by degrees or learning, charisma or leadership skill.

They are those who make glad the heart of God and they are identified by their incorruptible heart!

To be identified by nothing else than an incorruptible heart for God.

REFLECTION

1. When considering those Sauls who are still struggling, do you stand only in condemnation and judgement or do you sincerely and fervently pray for their restoration and healing?

2. Are there Sauls going through their Gethsemanes you can encourage forward?

3. Can you think of people who have the obvious favour of God on their lives due to the integrity of their heart yet they do not appear as gifted as some others?

4. What is more important to you – the acclaim of others or the commendation of the King?

5. What would you say is the driving force of your life?

PRAYER

This prayer is from George Warnock.

> *Lord, how we need the power and authority of Heaven to minister to the needs of suffering humanity, and to deliver your sheep that have been scattered and bruised in the wilderness of life.*
>
> *But Lord! Do not, we pray, place in our trust any measure of authority and power that is not counterbalanced with an equal measure of grace, and humility, and meekness,*

and patience, and kindness, and longsuffering, and mercy, and wisdom.

Keep this power and authority in Thine own hands, we pray, as the sword of Goliath was taken out of the hands of David, wrapped in a priestly garment, and hidden away in the Sanctuary till he was prepared of God to have it permanently and use it wisely.

Continue to hold us in the hollow of Thy hand as a sharp sword, to be used of Thee at Thy discretion.

Continue to polish us like the shaft of the arrow and keep us in Thy quiver, that when Thou dost see fit to send us forth, we shall not miss the mark, but we shall strike through the heart of the enemy unerringly.

Keep Thy power unto Thyself alone, for Thine is the Kingdom and the Power and the Glory. And may we only partake of it as we come into harmony and union with Thyself. Amen!

Final Thoughts

Although written in the KJV dialogue of his day, the words of Warnock still hold power today. It is my prayer and I trust yours also, that a year from now and a decade or two from now, we will still run this race with a sense of His pleasure.

As I have contemplated my own humanity and that gravitational pull towards Saul, I have at times, felt that tremor of insecurity as I have been confronted in some way by my frailty. That, I think, is common to us all.

However, what rises quickly to meet it is that deep held conviction within me, that as I walk in intimacy with His heart and maintain my passion to serve Him, it is the ever present Person of the Holy Spirit who will empower me to honour Him.*My responsibility is not to strive for perfection but to maintain the intimacy of my heart with His. How beautifully simple it really is!

Never doubt the reality of His love for you and never doubt His unqualified joy at receiving the love that you communicate to Him. He is your Father and fathers gain enormous pleasure from having their children share their lives with them. The fact He is your undisputed King and all you are is subject to Him, will never complicate the sheer delight He feels when you joyously serve Him out of sheer love and love alone.

Bibliography

Basham, D. 1973. True & False Prophets. Greensburg, Pennsylvania: Manna Books.

Cole, Dr. E. 1987. Lecture on leadership. Seattle, Washington.

Damazio, F. 1988. The Making of a Leader. Portland, Oregon: City Christian Publishing.

Mumford, R. 1987. Lecture on leadership. Portland, Oregon.

Myra, H., and Shelley, M. 2005. The Leadership Secrets of Billy Graham. Grand Rapids, Michigan: Zondervan.

Sanders, J. O. 1986. Spiritual Leadership, 10th ed. Kent, England: Send the Light Trust.

Warnock, G. 1987. In Wilkerson, D. The Refiner's Fire (A journal for those who seek a fuller revelation of the Lord Jesus Christ), Volume One. First Ed. Russellville, Arkansas: Storm Harvest.

Wiwcharuck, P. 1973. Christian Leadership Development and Church Growth. Fort Washington, Pennsylvania: Christian Literature Crusade.

About

DAVID McCRACKEN
MINISTRIES

David McCracken is recognized as a Prophet & Teacher who walks with integrity and godly character. In a day where gifts can often cover a lack of Christ-like character, David believes that there is no substitute or shortcut for a personal and intimate relationship with God. David is received in an Apostolic role to many individuals and Churches. He has dedicated the remaining years of his life to identifying and sowing into merging Prophets and ministers and being a prophetic voice to the Body of  Christ. David has been married to Margaret for over 40 years and they have three grown children and six grandchildren. David & Margaret make their home in Melbourne, Australia.

The mission of David McCracken Ministries is to be a prophetic ministry that empowers the Church. Our vision is to identify, develop, and release a prophetic team that ministers globally, and establish a ministry centre to empower the Church (through training) and restore the broken (through a ministry retreat). We do this by communicating the heart of God accurately and with integrity, and our team minister regularly, develop empowering resources, and run courses throughout the year. We highly value our partners and you can find out more at www.DavidMcCracken.org where you can signup for our monthly eNews and see how to get involved.

Other Resources by David McCracken

Overcomers - This is a series by David McCracken designed to impart keys to spiritual authority into the life of every Christian. The victory has already been won, now it's up to us to walk in it - you won't want to miss one second of this truly empowering series.

Leaders of Destiny - A seminar run by David McCracken to raise up a generation of leaders whose character foundations will support and not crumble under the weight of their gifting and charisma. A truly inspiring course!

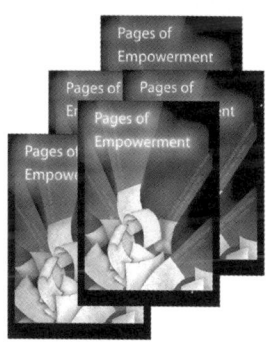

Pages of Empowerment - A truly inspiring devotional booklet series designed to bring God's people out of the shadows and into the light of their greater potential. John Bevere states "Pages of Empowerment is a wonderful book to bring hope, courage, and strength to all. I found life being released into my heart!"

For more resources, our ministry itinerary and other information about our ministry, please visit us online:
www.DavidMcCracken.org.
You may also email us:
info@davidmccracken.org
or write to:
PO Box 816, Endeavour Hills, VIC, 3802, Australia.